THE
GREATNESS
WITHIN
YOU

THE GREATNESS WITHIN YOU

BELIEVE IN YOURSELF AND DISCOVER YOUR POTENTIAL

LES BROWN

MEDIA

MEDIA

Published 2021 by Gildan Media LLC
aka G&D Media
www.GandDmedia.com

First Edition: 2021

Front cover design by David Rheinhardt of Pyrographx

Interior design by Meghan Day Healey of Story Horse, LLC.

Library of Congress Cataloging-in-Publication Data is available upon request

ISBN: 978-1-7225-0508-0

10   9   8   7   6   5   4   3   2   1

CONTENTS

1

BELIEVE IN YOURSELF

You have greatness within you. Yes, that's right. You have greatness within you. I want you to tell yourself this every day: I have greatness within me. Say it with conviction. I have greatness within me. Yes, you do.

This book is designed to help you tap into your greatness, and it's going to impact every area of your life. It's going to impact you on a personal level. If you apply its lessons, you're going to enhance your relationship with yourself, with your family members, with your friends, the people you work with, and your customer base. This book is going to bring out a part of you that you've had glimpses of, but never really lived.

Greatness. Greatness is choice. It's not your destiny, and you have to be mindful. You have to do certain things in certain way. There's a ritual you have to engage in in order to step into your greatness. I want you to think about things that you want to achieve with your life. I want you first of all to focus on your personal life. I want you to think about what are some of the things that you know about yourself that you know you need to work on, that you know you need to develop—the things that, if you get them right, will allow your life to move on to another level.

Don't try to do everything at the same time. Start by focusing on one area of your life that you know you need to work on right now. Like the lady said, "Lord, ain't what we going to be, ain't what I'm going to be, but thank God I sure ain't what I was."

When I look at my life and I look back at the goals I wanted to achieve, I think of my mentor, Mike Williams. He said to me, "Les, what is it you want to achieve?" I told him that I wanted to be involved in speaking, to help and inspire other people. But I didn't have the money, didn't have the education, and I had no experience of doing it. And it's a very competitive field.

He said to me, "Les, I want you to start by looking at *you*. What is it you need to change about you? What do you have to work on? As you think about that, I want to ask you a question. If you had your life to live over again, what would you do differently? I want you to think about that, too. What is one area of your life that, you know, if you worked on it, if you got that together, your life would change?"

For me it was overcoming my lack of self-confidence, not believing in myself. I had a tremendous inferiority complex because I don't have a college education, and I didn't think I could compete with people like Tony Robbins and Dr. Norman Vincent Peale, Robert Schuller and Zig Ziglar, and the other big names on the speaking circuit. I didn't believe I had what it takes to become an intellectual resource for corporate America.

Because of my lack of belief in myself, I hadn't taken any steps toward achieving my goal. What I want to ask yourself is: what regimen do I have to build myself up? As you think about the goals you want to achieve in your personal life and in your professional life, what is it about you that has to change? How do you need to begin to train your mind to serve you?

Most of don't realize how we are affected by the things we hear, what we are told, by the rejections we face. We live in a world where we're told more about our limitations than our potential, so most people go through life operating on a level of mediocrity. Most people never discover their greatness. I think that's why one woman asked, in a moment of anguish, "What if you live your life only to discover that it was wrong, that you're living somebody else's lie?" I know in my own life I'll never forget that as a child I was labeled "educable mental retarded" and put back from the fifth to the fourth grade. I failed again in the eighth grade.

I was called DT in school. DT stands for Dumb Twin. I have a twin brother, Wesley, who is very smart. And my sister Margaret graduated from the University of Miami with honors. But I didn't have college training. Being called DT, Dumb Twin, caused me to buy into that characterization. That affected me, set me back in life. There's a line in the movie *Magnolia* that I'll never forget. The character played by Tom Cruise says, "We might be through with our past, but our past is not through with us."

What is affecting you that you perhaps aren't even aware of? I had no idea, on a conscious level, how being called the Dumb Twin and people having low expectations for me affected my childhood and even my personal relationships. I was adopted, and I didn't realize that deep down I had a belief that if my mother didn't want me, it would be just a matter of time before other people would reject me.

Because I didn't feel deserving, I conducted myself in such a way that caused others to reject me. I didn't feel deserving, and so I was working against myself. One of the things that I want you to do is to spend time thinking about you and writing down some of your thoughts, such as your goals and your vision of yourself, what you want to achieve in your personal life, in your relationships with other people.

As you think about that, I want you to write down a detailed description of the kind of person you must become in order to produce the results you want in your personal life. Why? Because you don't get what you want in life by wanting it. What you *are* is what gets you what you want in life. What has to change about you as you look at yourself, as you develop a relationship with yourself, spending time with yourself through prayer, meditation, reading, developing yourself, training yourself? What is it as you look at yourself that you need to do that will make a radical change and a shift in the way in which you show up in life?

Why am I paying so much attention to the personal stuff? Because I have found that if you are suffering on a personal level, if your personal relationships are not working out fine, if you don't have a good relationship with yourself, if you don't have a good relationship with the people in your circle, your family members and friends, or your significant other, it's going to spill over into your professional results. The way in which you show up each and every day, the money that you earn, takes a great deal of mental stamina.

It takes a belief in *you*. It takes a passion. It takes a drive to face rejections day in and day out. Think of a doctor who looks through you rather than examining you, not wanting to pay attention to you, who is more concerned about himself and doesn't even serve the interests of his patients, who will not extend you the courtesy of listening to you, which of course is something that could enhance his practice and better serve his patients. He doesn't give you the time of day. In order for that not to take you out of the game, in order for that to not cause you to throw in the towel and become frustrated, you've got to be grounded and rooted in every dimension of yourself. I want you to have an intention, a mindset of taking care of yourself.

I read something by Ian Levenson. "Give to yourself until your cup runneth over, and then give to others from the overflow." I know that's right, and so I want you to become involved in a ritual, a program of giving to yourself. I love music. Do you like music? I love to dance. I love having good conversations. I love to read. I want you to have a ritual of things that you're going to do to give to yourself first, and then to give to others from the overflow; a program for yourself.

Now here's the other thing. I want you to think about the goals that you want to achieve for increasing your sales, for example. This is going to be the most incredible year you've ever had. Yes, that you've ever had. Yes, you. If this is going to be a breakthrough year, you want to have a mindset, an intention, of breaking your own record, of surprising yourself, and you can do that. When you set your mind to it, when you make the commitment that this is it for me, then you're going to break through.

Right now, just pat yourself on the back and say, "Goodbye." That's right. Pat yourself on the back and say goodbye. Why? Because in order to do something you've never done, you've got to become someone you've never been. I want you to think about the goals that you want to achieve, and whatever those goals are on a personal level and on a professional level, the number of sales, the kind of revenue that you want to generate, I want you to go beyond those goals.

Now I want to warn you. Don't ask yourself how you're going to do it. How is none of your business. You've got greatness within you. You have the ability to pull on and to tap into some things in you right now that you don't even know exist. Don't try and engage the rational mind on this. This is no place for the rational mind. Just trust me on this. As you think about your goals and dreams, I want you to know that it's possible to achieve them. I'm saying that based on my own experience.

If any negative thoughts creep into your mind and say to you that you can't do it, that those goals are just too ambitious, here's how I snap myself into reality, and I want you to do the same thing. Just say, "Barack." That's all you need to say, "Barack." Every time you think that you can't do something, that it's a long shot, just say, "Barack."

Now, I'll let you think about that for a while. You can do some things right now that you don't even know. If in the past anybody had told me that I would be talking to you right now, given my circumstances, born on the floor of an abandoned building with my twin brother, I wouldn't have believed it. If my birth parents came to me right now and tapped me on the shoulder and said, "Hello, son," I would not know either one of them. If anybody had told me that I have the capacity to earn millions of dollars doing what I love to do, I wouldn't have believed it. But it happened. I don't mention this to impress you, but to impress upon you that you have greatness within you.

What's possible for one is possible for all. Yes, you have to tap yourself on the back and say, "Good-bye." Why? Because in order to accomplish the goals and do something you've never done, you've got to become someone you've never been. You've got to die to who you are now to give birth to the person you can become, and you're going to. As you read this, some of you right now can feel me in your mind and in your heart. You know I'm right. You keep on reading, and one day you're going to wake up. You're going to look in the mirror, and a different person is going to be looking back at you.

You're going to be in situations that you will master. You're going to command the respect of professional people, of your customers. You're going to track sales. Doors will be open that you hadn't even seen before, just because of the way in which you show up, and who you are when you step into the place—because you will be emanating a level of power and presence and greatness that will compel them to do business with you. You have greatness within you.

Decide what your mindset will be and put the agenda in your mind. When you alone, and not the rest of the world, will determine your mindset, then the possibilities are unlimited. See, out of intention comes commitment. Goethe said, "Until one is committed, there is hesitancy, the chance to draw back, always ineffectiveness. Concerning all acts of initiative and creation, there is one elemental truth, the ignorance of which kills countless ideas and splendid plans: that the moment one commits oneself, then Providence moves too. All sorts of things occur to help one that would never have otherwise occurred. A whole stream of events issues from the decision, raising in one's favor all manner of unforeseen incidents and meetings and material assistance, which no man could have dream would have come his way. Whatever you can do, or dream you can, begin it. Boldness has genius, power, and magic in it. Begin it now."

Yes. When you make a commitment to do something, things happen. Something happens when you set your mind to it. There's a reason that Ralph Waldo Emerson said, "What lies behind us and what lies before us is of small consequence to what lies within us." While other people are focused on the competition, while other people are focused on the apathy of doctors, while other people are focused on the lack of resources and all the negative things out there that they think will justify them not stepping up to the next level and performing at a high level, you focus on developing your greatness. Trust me on this. As you begin to look at yourself and work on yourself, there's nothing that you cannot overcome.

That's why Elsie Robinson said, "Things may happen around you and things may happen to you, but the only things that really count are the things that happen in you." In you each and every day must be an intention that this is my day. This is going to be an incredible day and I am the person that's going to create some incredible business. You must have that kind of mindset. That's how you must come in. You must show up like that. That must be your intention and your mindset. That kind of spirit will make a place for you.

I remember once preparing myself to venture into an arena that I had never been in before, an arena that would be filled with people who had more money and education and contacts than me, and relationships and resources that I did not have. And as I was trying to answer the question, "How can I do this?" I came across something that Henry David Thoreau wrote. "I have learned this, that if you advanced confidently in the direction of your dreams and endeavor to live the life which you have imagined, you will meet with a success unexpected in common hours. You will put some things behind. You will pass an invisible boundary: new, universal, and more liberal laws will begin to establish themselves around and within you, or the old laws will be expanded and interpreted in your favor in a more liberal sense. You will live with the license of a higher order of beings."

Trust me on this. When you set the goals that you want to achieve in your personal life, taking care of your spiritual life, taking care of your health, there's something that happens that it's hard for the logical, practical, rational mind to understand. Case in point: I experienced something that no one ever wants to experience, to hear the words, "You have cancer." Those are three words that are the most feared words in many different languages. "You have cancer," and what I had to do immediately was to go within myself and say,

"How am I going to deal with this? Do I have cancer or does cancer have me?"

I saw it as a project, and I began to say with confidence that "I am more powerful than cancer. I'm going to conquer this." And I have. My PSA, which stands for prostate specific antigen, was over 700. One to four is normal. Because I study the area of psychoneuro-immunology, I know that what you believe affects you on a cellular level. When you have an intention of what it is you want to create, it's amazing what you can produce.

I'm cancer-free as a result of the mindset that I'm more powerful than cancer. You are more powerful than the rejections that you will face each and every day. You have the power to build relationships in your personal life, and a relationship with yourself, to take care of your health. Why is that important? Because you've got to show up, you've got to have stamina, you've got to cover a lot of territory, you've got to have a good energy and a good mindset and a good vibration when you are involved in business or any other activity. Every day you've got to be on.

There is no place for slackers. Ninety-nine and a half won't cut it, you've got to give 100 percent. You've got to bring it from down deep. What matters most is *you*. The real key to your success is you. If you have all the things that were working against you now working for you, that would be great, but if you don't use the resources that you have, if you don't show up and believe that you are the one, you won't win. The tools alone won't win for you. You have to win. The products won't win for you. The studies won't win for you. You have to win. The buck stops with you.

Yes, it's possible. In spite of circumstances, in spite of how things may have changed, you can win today. If you take care of yourself personally, and have a game plan and a ritual, and a regimen that you're living to achieve an integrated life, then you can reach your goals. Taking care of yourself and your personal relationships—emotionally, spiritually, and physically, gives you a game plan of how you're going to keep yourself balanced and be on top of everything. When you get up in the morning, have an intention of what it is you want to achieve that day. Work out your agenda the night before, what it is you're going to get out of the day, and while others are just trying to get through the day, it's possible that you can reach your goals.

Not only is it possible for you to reach your goals— for example, that you can make sales in spite of the economy—but it's necessary that you begin to understand that it's you, that you have to reinvent yourself, that you have to raise the bar on yourself, that you have to hold yourself accountable. You have to hold yourself to a higher standard. It's necessary that you have a deep-down resolve that "I'm going to make this happen." Raise the bar on yourself.

I once read that "If you only achieve those things that you know you can achieve, you rob yourself of life's greatest moments." Raise the bar on yourself. Challenge yourself. I've found that most people fail in life not because they aim too high and miss, but because they did what I did for so many years: I aimed too low. You've got greatness in you. Yes, I'm talking to you. You have greatness within you.

2

SET GOALS

I want you to think about the major goals that you'd like to achieve in your life. I want you to think about them in three areas. Number one, what's one personal goal you have that you'd like to achieve? Two, what is some financial goal that you'd like to achieve, some business goal that you'd like to achieve? Some social goal is the third one. Horace Mann said, "We should be ashamed to die until we have made some major contribution to humankind." What will be different because you were born? What will be different for you?

My first major goal was to buy my mother a home. I'm adopted. I'm one of seven children that my mother adopted. I was born in the poor section of Miami, Florida called Liberty City, in an abandoned building, on the floor with my twin brother. When we were six weeks of age, we were adopted by Mrs. Mamie Brown.

I wanted to take care of my mother. My mother was a domestic worker on Miami Beach. She was a determined person with a great deal of drive, a great deal of passion for what she did. We ate the food left over from the families that she cooked for. These were very kind and generous people. They would say, "Mamie, whatever food is left over after we eat, you pack it up and take it home to those seven children that you have adopted." We wore the hand-me-down clothes of the children that mama looked after. Mama could sew, and if the clothes were too small she would take them out. Too large, she would take them in. And my mama could bake, too. My mama would bake us sweet potato pie so good that you couldn't eat it with your shoes on. Yeah, you took your shoes off so you could wiggle your toes.

And so I said, "Mama, when I become a man, I am going to buy you a big beautiful home just like the one you work at." She worked for a family that had a 10,000-square foot mansion on Miami Beach with a swimming pool. That was my fantasy, to buy her a house like that. That was the goal. Do you have somebody special that you'd like to do something special for? I'm sure you do. Now, I want you to think about that. I want you to think about that person who has blessed you. As I write this I'm thinking about a gentleman who's been a blessing in my life. I've been working with him and I look forward to talking with him when I go back to Miami to visit him. His name is Mr. Leroy Washington, and he changed my life. He's a teacher. I was in his classroom one day working, waiting for another student. He said, "Young man, go to the board and work this problem out for me." I said, "Sorry, sir. I can't do that." "Why not?" he asked me, I replied, "Sir, I'm not one of your students." He said, "Look at me." "Yes, sir," I said. "Go to the board and work that problem out anyhow." I said, "Sir, I can't." "Why?" "Sir, because I'm educable mentally retarded," and the students in the classroom started laughing.

As the students were laughing, they said, "He's DT." Mr. Washington said, "What does that mean?" "He's the dumb twin. That's Leslie, not Wesley." And I said, "They're right, sir." He came from behind his desk, looked at me and said, "Don't ever say that again. Someone's opinion of you does not have to become your reality." That was a turning point in my life. On one hand, I was humiliated. But on the other hand, I was liberated. Because he looked at me with the eyes of Goethe, who said, "Look at a man the way he is and he only becomes worse, but look at him as if he were what he could be, then he becomes what he should be."

Now, I want to ask again, do you have major goals you want to achieve? And I want to ask you another key question. Do you know that if you had your life to live over again, you could've done more than what you've accomplished thus far? What we do and what we accomplish in life is only a tip of the iceberg of what's possible for us. All of us have something special. We all have greatness within ourselves.

There are three primary reasons that I've found that lead to most people getting stuck in life. Number one I that most people don't know what they have going for them. This Les Brown here, for years I held him back; for 14 years, in fact. I held myself back because I did not know the truth about myself. I was in bondage. I was living a life of mediocrity. We live in a world where we're told more about our limitations than our potential.

Have you have gone through some stuff that still affects you in the present? Many of those things can impact our lives, without our being conscious of it. I used to go see Zig Ziglar and Dr. Norman Vincent Peale, who wrote the *Power of Positive Thinking.* They would say that you have something special. You have greatness in you. Don't allow your negative thoughts to hold you back. Don't allow your circumstances to determine who you are. When Dr. Peale spoke, it gave me goose pimples.

I remember one of my goals and dreams was to share a platform with him, and I finally had the chance to do that in Kentucky. Og Mandino couldn't make the engagement and so I showed up there and when I got to the back door I said to the person who opened it, "Hi. My name is Les Brown."

The person replied, "But you're not the band leader." I said, "No. I'm not." "Well, who are you?" So I told him, "I'm Mrs. Mamie Brown's favorite boy." He looks at me for a moment and then says, "Well, who is Mamie Brown?" I said, "My mama." Anyway, he took me to Dr. Peale's dressing room.

When I got there Dr. Peale's wife said to him, "Les Brown is here. He is not the band leader. It's Les Brown." Dr. Peale's back was to me and he said, "Les Brown? Shoot for the moon because even if you miss, you will land among the stars, that Les Brown?"

I replied, "Sir, that's my quote. I sent that to you when I was in the 11th grade. I wrote that for a contest. You remember that?"

"Yes, Mr. Brown. I end every speech with that quote." He had thought it was from the band leader Les Brown, of Les Brown and the Band of Renown.

I used to go see Zig Ziglar, the number one motivational speaker on the planet. He and Tony Robbins dominate the industry. I also went to see Mark Victor Hansen, another icon, and Jack Canfield and Jim Rohn.

My heart would say *I could do that*. And then my mind would ask, *Les Brown, how would you do that?* I didn't have a college education. How would I speak to AT&T, Procter & Gamble, McDonald's, IBM, Xerox? I'd never worked for a major corporation. As a child I was labeled "educable mentally retarded." *You don't even know who your parents are. You were put back from the fifth grade to the fourth grade, then failed again in the eighth grade.* How many of you ever thought about something you wanted to do and then talked yourself out of it?

There's an African proverb that says if there's no enemy within, the enemy outside can do us no harm. For 14 years I procrastinated. For 14 years I was on the sidelines. For 14 years I just watched; I was silent. I once spent a day with Maya Angelou, and she said something I just love. "Most people go so far in life and then they park," she said. I know why most people park. I had a goal and a dream of having a talk show. But it was canceled. I took a hit, and I parked. I was married to someone and I thought we would be married for the rest of our lives, but we got divorced. I took a hit, and I parked again. My mother, my rock, was diagnosed with breast cancer. I parked. I was diagnosed with prostate cancer and given two to three years to live. That was 14 years ago. My best friend died waiting for a liver transplant. I took so many hits, and each time I parked. I didn't turn my emergency lights on because I didn't want to call attention to myself. I just parked.

Have you ever been parked like that? People go to jobs they hate and at the same time they hope they don't get fired. That's what you call mixed emotions. I was parked. And so I would go to seminars, go workshops, I was reading books. I was listening to motivational messages. I would see people doing what I wanted to do and my conversation with myself, the story I told myself was *you can't do that*. I convinced myself that I couldn't do it. Most people are stuck because they don't know what they have going for them. I did know what I had going for me, but I only focused on the things I had working against me.

Here's the other reason that most people are stuck. Most people don't know how to make money with their gift. I had the ability to speak but I didn't know how to make money with my talent. I know people who know how to write but they don't know how to make money with their writing. I know people who have business skills, consulting skills, coaching skills—all types of ideas, talent, abilities, and specialized knowledge, but they don't know how to make money with them. Most people don't know how to make money with what they have going for them.

Here's the third reason that most people don't know how to get ahead, and that is that they don't know how to get access to the people who will pay them for what they know. Am I correct? So those are three reasons why people are stuck. One, they don't know what they have going for them. Two, they don't know how to make money with what they have going for them. Three, they don't know how to get access to the people who will pay them for what they know.

The training that we provide can give you some things that people can use right away. Seth Godin, who has been called the world's greatest marketer, said something very interesting. "Becoming successful in business is about marketing, and marketing is not about making stuff. Marketing is about telling your story."

Write this down: *learn how to tell your story*. I want to give you some things that you can use right now. See, life really boils down to stories. I started off by telling you my story. I told you that I was born on the floor of an abandoned building in the poorest section of Miami, Florida, a place called Liberty City. My mama only had a third-grade education. She was a domestic worker on Miami Beach. Why did I tell you this?

Let me share some things with you right now. When you're speaking to someone and you're talking about your business, or your idea, your proposal, your invention, there are three questions in their minds, and you want to answer each of them. Number one, who are you? Number two, what do you have? And number three, why should I care? Now, most people don't answer those questions, and if you don't answer them in the course of your presentation you aren't going to win over the people you're presenting to.

Write this down: *people do business with people they know, like, and trust.* It's very important right from the start to let them know who you are, so they can decide "Is this somebody that I want to do business with?" Tell them who you are so that they answer "yes" to the question.

In your business, your ability to tell your story will allow you to achieve national and international branding—and I'm not saying this because I believe it, I'm saying it because I know. It will allow you to earn millions of dollars. This is what most people neglect. Most people spend very little time learning how to tell their story. We know about Mary Kay because Mary Kay knew the power of telling her story, about being passed over for promotion many times until she got sick and tired of it. She decided to start her own company and she told the story about the person that she brought the products from and how his hands looked so young and fresh, and about the products he was making and creating. She created a whole business around this concept, to empower women by telling her story. If you can just tell your story—I'll give you some steps that you can use right now to do that.

I want you to think about your goals, think about the personal goal you want to achieve, your professional goal, and your contribution to society. What will be different if you achieve it? What will your mark be? What will your legacy be? You have something special. You have greatness within you. You have the ability to do more than you can even begin to imagine. You have something in you that you need to work to unleash. Once you do, the world will never be the same again. You have this in you, you have books in you, you have leadership in you, you have genius in you, you have miracle-working power in you.

Now, let me share something with you. As you begin to look at your goals and dreams, say to yourself, "it's possible." Write that down: *it's possible.*

The easiest thing that I do is get up and speak. The most difficult thing that I've ever done, given my beginning—born on the floor of an abandoned building, being in poverty—the most difficult thing that I've ever done is to believe that I could do it. That's the most difficult part. It's possible. And write this down: *expand your vision.* Whatever your goals are that you set for yourself, your personal goals, your financial goals, your contribution to society, what your mark will be—expand it. I have found that most people fail in life not because they aim too high and miss. They fail because they did just like I did for 14 years. They aimed too low, and many don't aim at all. If you don't know where you're going, you're going to end up someplace else.

We are not taught by our educational system that we have greatness within us, that we have the ability to do more. By the way, to prove that you have greatness within you, consider the fact that you were the chosen one out of 400 million sperm. You have something in you that the world needs. There's something you brought here that was not here before you showed up. They say the two most important moments in our life are the day we are born and the day we realize why we were born. George Bernard Shaw was asked: If you had it in your power—here's a man that was very famous for his contribution, for his for his genius—if you had it in your power to be born again and to be anyone in history, who would you like to be?" To this he said, "I'd like to become the man I never was."

Wow. I'd like to become the man I never was. Now I understand the words of the woman who said, "Oh God, to reach the point of death only to realize that you've never lived; only to realize that you've never scraped the surface of your potential." I now understand those words. When I look at my life now, I see that what I thought I was at certain times in the past was not all that I could become. What I'm doing now is the result of people seeing something in me that I didn't see in myself. Now I understand that person who asked in a moment of anguish, "What if you lived your whole life only to discover that it was wrong?" I was wrong for the first part of my life. The majority of my life I was living small because I was not in a community of achievers. Because rather than having an expanded vision of myself, I had a limited vision of myself.

C-E-O. You are the CEO of your own life and destiny. C stands for the community of achievers, E stands for expanded vision, and O stands for optimistic mindset. I once suffered from "possibility blindness." I was stuck. I just couldn't see myself living the life that I'm now living. And here's why it's important that you learn how to discover your power voice, to tell your story: it will free you up to do some things that you don't know you can do right now. I am going to show you this not to impress you but to impress upon you what the possibilities are. As you begin to look at your goals and your dreams, I want you to just run you through a process. I want you to think about what your goals are right now and what you want to achieve. Now, what I did was I resigned from the Ohio legislature. I went back home to take care of my mother. My goals have changed now. My original goals were to start my own business, to become financially independent, and to take care of my mother.

I was a state legislator when my mother was diagnosed with breast cancer. She became a 22-year breast cancer conqueror. I gave up my political ambitions and I went back home to take care of my mama. I had a problem when my brother called me and said, "We're going to put mama in a nursing home." I said, "Why?" He replied, "Because she can't take of herself." I said, "No, no, no, no. We're not going to do that. We're going to take care of her."

My brother replied, "We thought you would say that, Leslie, and we interviewed a lot of people, and the people we chose are going to be really nice, really take care of her."

I said, "Let me tell you something. She didn't clean their behinds. She cleaned our behinds." I couldn't understand how one woman could raise seven children when they couldn't take care of themselves, but seven grown people couldn't take care of one woman. I had a problem with that.

That was at a very difficult time in my life and there are people that are going through things right now. Going through some tough times in their lives and giving up on themselves. Let me just say this. There are some things you can't see looking forward that you can only see looking back. Those tough times for me gave birth to a Les Brown that I did not know existed. Everything happens for a reason. One of my favorite quotes is "Many times in life when we have a teeth-rattling experience and the very foundation of our life has been shaken, we run to God only to discover that it's God that's doing the shaking."

At another point in my life I was a disc jockey. No one could've told me then that I would be doing what I'm doing right now. My conversation with myself, the story that told myself, was that I was a disc jockey. Many people live their lives as a result of a story they believe about themselves. That's was me. A disc jockey is what I thought I was. I was on that track. And I did it very well. Now, I can go into a city, you give me a microphone, I'll turn it upside down. They call me Les Brown, the man about town who will tell you that story, and explain how you can strategically tell a story and create an experience that can change people's opinion about your business, your product, or your service. It's amazing. Remember, this is very important to becoming a strategic communicator. I'm sure you want to learn how to that too, and this book will teach you.

I'm sure many of you reading this want to change your lives. I am going to show you how a particular gentleman changed my life, and how I now have this thing figured out. I have mastered this. I'm going to teach you how to do it; something you can do right now. When you are talking with people who you're trying to help or want to work with, be it young people or adults, do the following. Now write this down: *distract, dispute and inspire*. Distract, dispute, and inspire.

One day Mike Williams from Coshocton, Ohio, a dropout from Ohio State, said to me: "Les Brown, you are more than a disc jockey."

"What are you talking about, Mike?" I said to him. "Hold it just a minute, okay?" I put a record on the turntable and told the audience, "Look out ladies and gentlemen. Here comes Wilson Pickett, coming on with his souls. Pickett, come on. Kick it Pickett. Turn on your souls, Pickett." Then I turned back to Mike. "Now, what were you saying, Mike?"

"Les, you can be more than a disc jockey. If you can motivate people to go to the Jamaica Club or the Bottoms Up Club or the Pink Pussycat, you can talk to them about how to begin to deal with problems in the community, how to begin to address issues that are affecting them on a day-to-day basis."

"Hold it just a minute Mike, okay? Folks, here comes Aretha Franklin. Come on, Riri. Oh yeah, she's got a new thing called *Respect*. Come on, sock it to me, sock it to me, sock it to me. Come on, Riri baby. All right! I'm your man about town, Les Brown." I looked over at Mike. "Go ahead. What were you saying, Mike?"

"Les, let me tell you something, man. You can do more than this. You have the ability to touch people's lives. You are more than just an entertainer." With that, Mike Williams distracted me. *Distract*. He also *disputed* in that conversation through the way he told the story and painted a vision of a brighter future for me. He was calling on me to begin to see some of the possibilities.

And look at what happened to me. I became a state legislator. I was elected to the Ohio legislature and I got 14 bills passed in my first term. It gets funnier. Think of two little boys eating sugarcane. My brother and I were born with sugar cane in our mouths. If you had a choice between eating a silver spoon or eating sugar cane, what would you eat? Sugarcane, of course. And that's what I'm talking about. I'm telling you: you have greatness within you. Have you seen *Lion King*? Remember that line, "Simba, you are more than what you have become." Remember that line?

I wanted to be on stage with Dr. Norman Vincent Peale. I wanted to speak with him on stage. And I did. Who'd have thought one of the little boys eating sugarcane would appear with Dr. Phil and Dr. Phil would quote him? I don't write this to impress you, but what if I had been just a disc jockey? I wouldn't have worked for the National Speakers Association, the largest professional speakers association in the world. What if this guy, Mike Williams, had not spoken to me? Some of you may have gotten ideas that you have already shut down; you need to pull them out. How many of you ever heard of Toastmasters? Or the Golden Gavel Award? That's the highest award Toastmasters gives out. Who would've thought that of two little boys in

Liberty City eating sugarcane, one of them would have that sugarcane turn into a microphone?

What if I had had more people in my ear than Mike Williams? I might have become the Les Brown I am today much sooner. I sat on the sidelines for 14 years. There's one area of my life that I regret, and I can't unscramble those eggs. There are some people who decided to do drugs because they didn't hear my voice. When I was going down the street and I'd see young men walking with their pants dragging down below their butt, that made me angry with myself because it happened on my watch. On my watch. When I see the incarceration rate going up, that bothers me. Part of what I'm doing in my social commitment, in honor of my mother, is to reduce the number of women who die from breast cancer. She was a 22-year breast cancer conqueror. Part of my goal before leaving the planet is to impact the lives of young people, to eradicate HIV, that hood-infected virus. I want to end the addiction-to-incarceration and death syndrome, teach these kids mindset development, effective communication skills, and how to dress like a prospect and not a suspect.

Now I want to discuss success strategies for making it in a global economy. Because we are in the era that the late Peter Drucker called the era of the three C's—accelerated change, overwhelming complexity, and tremendous competition. Most people don't know that soon two-thirds of the jobs in the United States will be permanent part-time jobs with no health benefits. And even if you're working, you got to do two and three jobs to get by. As you begin to look at yourself, as we begin to look at where we are, it's very important that people get the tools, have the support, have the relationships, and have access to the resources that will allow them to reinvent themselves.

This is the age of self-reliance. You've got to be willing to die to who you are now to give birth to who you can become. I must die daily. Being conformed to this world, being transformed by the renewing of your mind and the developing of your power voice, that's what I call it. Your ability to speak from your heart in order to impact people's minds and touch *their* hearts is what will change their behavior. What is important about our relationships? Let's call it OQP—Only Quality People.

Only quality people means the value of being in a community of achievers. Sydney Poitier wrote a book called *The Measure of a Man*. In it he said, "When you go for a walk with someone, something happens without being spoken." He went on to say, "Either you adjust to their pace or they adjust to your pace." Whose pace have you adjusted to? Dr. Dennis Kimbro said, "If you're the smartest one in your group, you need to get a new group."

You've got to look at your relationships and ask the question, "What is this relationship doing to me?" See, you can't shrink your wing to greatness. You have to expand your wing to greatness. The reason most people go to their graves with their greatness still in them is because they won't take a chance. They're playing it safe. They say, "I can't afford to do it." I say, "Hey, I can't afford not to do it." They ask, "How much will it cost?" You should say, "Well, how much will it cost me if I don't do it?" If I had listened to my friends, I would never have gone on a Greyhound bus to Ed Foreman's executive development seminar. I caught a Greyhound bus from Miami to Dallas, Texas, to go to that seminar. My friends said, "You are stupid. Why would you go, Leslie? You are spending the last of your money. Why would you go? You've spent all your money trying to keep mama alive. Why would you go, Leslie?"

"I've got to go," I told them. They replied, "Leslie, you can go back to your job at Sears. They have good benefits there." So I told them I couldn't make enough money working that job. Mama took care of us. She made a way out of no way. I was determined to make money on my dream. So I told them I was going. "What are you going to do?" they asked me. "I'm going to learn how to speak. I like to help people." Sometimes you've got to get up. You've got to change territory. You've got to make a decision. You've got to see that life is a fight for territory. Write that down.

That's right. Life is a fight for territory. And once you stop fighting for what you want, what you don't want will automatically take over. I can do 142 push-ups. I don't mention that to brag. I'm doing that to stay alive because exercise alone, being a cancer conqueror, reduces the chances of cancer recurring by 37 percent. My body took a hit from cancer. I don't think doctors should tell people they're terminally ill like they told me. What they should say is, "My knowledge and ability to help you has terminated." They are not God. And I found in my research that more people die from a doctor's prognosis than from the disease itself. Part of what I do is tell people "You are more powerful than cancer." When cancer has you and when you have it, you can kick its butt. I'm telling you what I know. My PSA, which stands for prostate specific antigen, was over 400. One to four is normal. But today I'm cancer free, I'm debt free, and drama free.

For me, PSA stands for me positively staying alive. Life is a fight for territory and once you stop fighting for what you want, what you don't want will automatically take over. You've got to fight for your health. You have to fight for your business. You have to fight for your relationships. Things are going to happen to you that you can anticipate. It's possible to do this.

Now say to yourself: *I can live my dream. It's necessary.* Say it to yourself with conviction, say it out loud: *it's necessary.*

If you're casual about your dream you will end up a casualty. You've got to fight for your dream. You've got to say, "This dream is necessary." Why? Because when you have a goal, when you have a dream, you will have tribulations. You're going to get a visit from Murphy's Law. Who's Murphy? Don't worry. He's waiting for you out there in the world.

Murphy's Law says that if anything can go wrong, it will, and at the worst possible moment. That's why only two percent of people live their dreams, because they don't know that you've got to fight for your dream. That it's not something that you would like to do. You've got to say, "This is necessary." Paul Robeson said, "I stand here for I can do no other. I have got to speak." There are some of you who've got to do what you're doing. As much as you have chosen it, it has chosen you. Let me digress for a moment. One of my colleagues in the National Speakers Association was traveling across Europe. At that time he was trying to find himself. He told me, "Soldiers boarded the train and woke up the sleeping passengers and asked "Where have you been? Why are you here and where are you going?"

And so ask yourself, where have I been with my life, with my dream, with my idea, with my invention?

With my talent, my gift, my skill? Where are you going with your life? Where are you going with this dream, this thing that just won't let you sleep? Everywhere you turn, it's there. It's there slapping you on the face saying, "Answer me. Bring me to life." Remember this: Live full, die empty. Write that down.

I love to recall the words of Dr. Howard Thurman, who wrote *Deep is the Hunger*, and who was an advisor to Mahatma Gandhi and Albert Schweitzer and Martin Luther King. When I had 238 radiation seed implants for my cancer, the doctors told me, "Mr. Brown, your PSA is rapidly increasing. Your cancer obviously has metastasized; it has gone beyond the capsule of your prostate and there is nothing we can do." When I heard that I remembered reading the words of Dr. Thurman, who wrote this: "The ideal situation for man or woman is to die with their family members praying with them as they cross over."

But then he went on to say: "But imagine, if you will be on your deathbed and standing around your bed the ghost of the dreams, the ideas, the abilities, the talents given to you by life but you, for whatever reason, you never pursued those dreams, you never acted on those ideas, we never heard your voice, we never saw your leadership, you never wrote that book, you never formed that task and there they are standing around your bed, looking at you with large angry eyes saying, 'We came to you and only you could have given us life and now, we must die with you forever.'" The question is, if you die today, what dreams, what ideas, what abilities, what inventions, what businesses, what leadership, what voice, what book, what artwork, what photography will die with you?

Myles Munroe, a great preacher from the Bahamas, said "The wealthiest place in the planet is not in the Middle East where there is oil in the ground; it's not in South Africa where there are diamond mines. The wealthiest place on the planet is the cemetery." There you will find potential never realized. Reminds me of the poet who said, "Many a flower has bloomed unceasingly and wasted sweetness among the cold desert air. Many talented and gifted persons have gone unnoticed. But because they had no result, because they were suffering from possibility blindness, they never gave themselves a chance to show the genius that they were chosen to show." Now say to yourself: It's possible. It's necessary. I detoxify my life.

Many people never achieve their goals because they have too many energy-draining critics in their lives that sap their energy. My favorite book says, "Death and life is in the tongue." If I say to you, "You can't do that," then somebody else can come along and say, "You can do it. You can do it. You can do it. You can do it." John H. Johnson, who founded *Ebony* magazine, created a $400 million empire in Chicago out of a $500 loan from his mother, and he fired his best friend. Somebody said to him, "Why did you fire your best friend?" He replied, "Because he told me I couldn't do it. I don't need anybody on my payroll to tell me that."

Every day I had to convince myself, I had to believe in Mike William's belief in me. Sometimes you have to believe in somebody's belief in you until your own belief kicks in. And I'm saying to you that the world needs you. We need you to believe in yourself. To believe in you dream. To not give up. To see it through. We need you when you get knocked down to get back up. We need you when others say, No, you can't get the loan. No, we don't want that book. No, we don't think that's a good idea. We need you to keep coming back again and again and again and again. That's how I got here.

3

LEARN TO BE UNREASONABLE

We need your dream. Don't you give up on that dream. You may ask, when will your dream happen? It will happen when it happens. When will a baby walk? It will walk when it walks, and some walk sooner than others. When will it talk? It will talk when it talks. That's when it happens. I'll tell you, I used to sleep on the floor of the Penobscot building in Detroit, Michigan, on the 21st floor. I used to bathe in the sink down the hall from my office. Security said, "Mr. Brown, the office managers would like to see you." So I went to see them. They told me, "Mr. Brown, this is an office complex. It's not a hotel, sir."

"What do you mean?" I said.

"At two o'clock in the morning the janitorial staff saw you running down the hall in your underwear and hiding in the closet, trying to escape them seeing you."

"I was just working late that night," I told them.

You see, during the good times, you put it in your pocket. During the tough times you put it in your heart. It was tough sleeping in my office. I had to get up early before my staff got there and say, "All right. We're going to make it happen today. Yes, indeed. This is the day. We're going to do it." I was talking to them and I was talking to myself to keep my spirits up. Sometimes you have to encourage yourself.

My brother once said to me, "Les Brown."

"Yes?" I replied. "Wesley, why you calling me by my name? You know my name."

"Well, Mr. Motivator?"

"Yes, what is it, Wesley?"

"What do you do?" he asks me.

"I'm a motivational speaker."

"Who are you going to motivate?"

"Corporations."

"Is that right? Do these people have a college education?"

"Yes. You know they do, Wesley."

"Do you have a college education?"

"No, I don't, Wesley, and you know it. What's your point?"

"And how much are you going to charge to talk to them?"

"A thousand dollars an hour, Wesley."

"A thousand dollars an hour. Have you ever done what it is you're going to motivate them to do?"

"No, I haven't, but I'm going to learn."

"Oh, you're going to practice on them?"

"Yes, Wesley."

"Have you ever earned a thousand dollars in a week?"

"You know I haven't."

"Oh, but now you're going to go and speak to corporations. You've never work for a corporation. These people have a college education and you have none, and they're going to reach other people, PhDs and MBAs, and they have years of experience and they're going to hire you to come in and motivate them at a thousand dollars an hour to do something you have never done."

"Yes, Wesley."

"You are crazy." Now write this down. *Learn to become unreasonable.* See, my brother was being practical and realistic.

You've got to learn how to be unreasonable. Entrepreneurs are unreasonable. For centuries mankind walked, then rode on the backs of animals. Then one day someone said, "Whoa. You know, I think we can fly like birds." But let's be reasonable; let's be logical. Let's be realistic. If God wanted people to fly, he'd have given them what? Wings, of course. We're not supposed to fly. One of the people who said that was a minister in Dayton, Ohio, who was a pastor there and the father of two sons. His two sons were the ones who made the first powered flight in an airplane. I'm talking about Wilbur and Orville Wright. Thank God, they didn't listen. Don't listen to the critics.

Don't listen to your critics. There's never been a statue erected to a critic. When I was a kid we used to say, "You got as much chance of doing that as a man going to the moon." We can't say that anymore. If you think your dream is a long shot, every time you're thinking that, you get mesmerized by that mind virus I call possibility blindness. This is the way you can snap yourself out of it: just say "Barack." That's how you snap yourself back. I don't care if you're an Independent, Democrat, or a Republican. If you think your dream is a long shot, just say, "Barack", and start working. You don't know what you can't do. You've got to be intelligently ignorant. According to the laws of aerodynamics, a bumblebee isn't supposed to fly because its little puny wings can't hold up its large body—but the bumblebee doesn't know that. He keeps on doing it anyhow.

I'll never forget a conversation I had with Mr. Washington, the teacher. He said, "Mr. Brown, what do you want to do with your life, young man?" I replied that I wanted to take care of my mama. He said, "How are you planning to do that? So I said that I'd like to become a disc jockey. Then he said, "You got to be hungry."

"Why do you say that?" I asked him.

Mr. Washington said, "People that are hungry are willing to do the things that others won't do in order to have the things tomorrow that others won't have. People that are hungry take risks—if you're not willing to risk, you cannot grow and if you cannot grow, you cannot become your best. And if you cannot become your best, you can't be happy, and if you can't be happy, then what else is there? I like what Helen Keller said: 'Life is short and unpredictable. Eat the dessert first.' You got to be hungry, young man."

"I am hungry, sir. I am hungry to take care of my mother. I'm hungry to make something of my life." All my life people had compared me to my brother Wesley. They would say, "You're not smart like Wesley." All my life I had heard people say, "Maybe take him back to the Welfare Department. He's got problems." All my life, people told me that I would not make it. They called me DT, the dumb twin.

Mr. Washington wasn't through talking to me. He said, "Mr. Brown, why were you in the Dean's office the other day?"

"For fighting, sir."

"Why were you fighting?"

"Because they called me DT."

"Mr. Brown, don't fight."

"Why, sir?"

"Because anger is the wind that blows out the lamp of the mind. Don't fight. Don't get angry."

"Then what should I do, sir? What should I do when they pick on me?"

"Mr. Brown, most people would rather get even than get hit. You have a good memory?"

"Yes sir, I do."

"I know you can't read well, but I see your lips moving when I speak. You memorize things quickly, don't you?"

"Yes, sir."

"Good. Remember these words from Frank Sinatra. 'The best revenge is massive success.' Focus on becoming massively successful. That's where you put your energy. That's where you put your time. Don't answer your critics. No, no, no. What they think about you is none of your business. You focus on becoming massively successful. I'm saying to you, focus on becoming massively successful. Focus on mastering yourself, focus on mastering the telling of your story, focus on mastering success."

It's a learning process. All of us are born the same way—dumb, naked, and speechless. No one comes in knowing anything. You must be willing to do the things that the others won't do in order to have the things tomorrow that others won't have. You are cut from a different cloth. You're a different kind of person. You are strange. You don't want to be like everybody else. You see a different life for yourself. You have said I can do better than this; this can't be it. That's what I said. I wanted a different life for myself, for my children. Say this: *You've got to be hungry.* You've got to be hungry.

"So what do you want to do, young man?" Mr. Washington asked me.

"I want to become a disc jockey."

"Is that right? Good, Mr. Brown. Here's what you do. Work on your mind. Listen to Earl Nightingale, *The Strangest Secret In The World*, Dr. Norman Vincent Peale, Zig Ziglar. Listen to their motivational messages on a regular basis. Program your mind. You don't get in life what you want; you get in life what you are. I suggest to you, take the time to read 10 to 15 pages of something positive every day. Take the time to listen to motivational messages. Review the lectures. Why? Faith comes by hearing and hearing and hearing. I do it to this day. I do it now. Why? Because you can't kill negative thoughts; they are like weeds. James Allen was right. There is no such thing as weed killer. You can keep them at bay for a while but you stop using it, they'll come back with a vengeance."

That's what happened to me. I got one of my goals, one of my dreams. I wanted a national syndicated show. I did all the things to get there and then I stopped doing those things. I used to watch the Phil Donahue show. And as I listened to him I said, "I want to have a show." And King World sponsored my show, paid me $5 million. I stopped reading, I stopped working on myself, I lost myself in what I was doing. I became so busy I didn't take care of me. I wasn't mastering me, and when they took me to Manhattan and had me in a $7,500 a month condo, and I had a security guard, and they were picking me up in a limousine, my mentor was saying to me, "Les, this is not the mountain top. There are no overachievers in the universe." And my conversation with myself was, "Whoa. This is too good to be true." Something was bound to happen and it did. It did.

I thought it was too good to be true. See, if your achievements exceed your own sense of self-worth, you will unconsciously engage in self-destructive behavior; take yourself out. I took myself out of the game. If there is no enemy within, the enemy outside can do us no harm. "The fault, dear Brutus, is not in our stars but in ourselves, that we are underlings." Abraham Lincoln said, "If I have eight hours to cut a tree down, I'll take six hours sharpening my ax." I'm telling you what I know. Master yourself.

"Got to be hungry, Mr. Brown," Mr. Washington told me. "Listen to Paul Harvey."

"Why, sir?" I asked.

"Because he is the world's greatest communicator. Whenever you want to do something Mr. Brown, watch what the masters do."

I used to watch Billy Graham with the volume down, watching his eyes. I watched how he used his stance. I studied Dr. Norman Vincent Peale and Zig Ziglar. I wanted to see what they were doing. The masters in your area, the people that are doing what it is that you want to do, you want to study them. You want to read their books. You want to go to their seminars. You want to watch them. You want to do your research and develop yourself so that you can do what they are doing, and then take it beyond that. I watch my competition. Make yourself stand out. Talk about your business, talk about your services, talk about your invention. Make yourself stand out.

I said to myself, "What is it that could make me stand out? I noticed something about my competitors. They are scripted. So what if I read two to three books a week? They won't do that. I've got to out-think them. I've got to outwork them. I don't have their credentials. I don't have their contacts. I don't have their money. But I can think. I can work. I can work to develop myself, to train myself to speak extemporaneously, to custom design my presentation. Start thinking like Henry David Thoreau: "The people that make it in this life, they look around for the circumstances that they want and if they can't find them, they create them."

Goals and dreams are achieved twice—once in the brain and then outside it. Being around a community of people, getting the tools and resources you need, expanding your vision and your opportunity mindset will drive your life to a new place. And in a historical context, the world will never be the same because you had the courage not to give up on your dream. You had the courage to fight for your dream. Fighting through tears, sometimes. Sometimes you run out of money and have no idea how you are going to make it. But you found a way. Sleeping on the floor of the Penobscot building, looking out the window and questioning myself, "Do I think I can do this? God, give me a sign. Did I make the right decision?" And then I realized that you won't get a sign. If you see it, it's not about faith. If you believe it, you'll see it. I had to hold the vision and you've got to hold your vision.

4

THE MOST INCREDIBLE TIME OF YOUR LIFE

I want to share with you something that I want you to begin to put your mind around. This is going to be the most incredible year you've ever had. That's right. The most incredible time of your life. I want you to know that the steps that I share with you are things you must do day in and day out. This is not something you do once in a while. It's every day. It's a ritual that you must engage in every day to create a breakthrough in your thinking.

Now I want you to understand about the power of words. Rudyard Kipling said, "Words are, of course, the most powerful drug used by mankind." Every year we see things in the media about how we need to protect ourselves, to inoculate ourselves, to protect ourselves from the seasonal flu. Let me share something with you, what you're doing in this process of reading my book. I affect you not only on the conscious level, but the subconscious level and the cellular level. When I speak to you through this book, there's a part of you that I'm speaking to that has more power and the ability to do things than you can ever begin to imagine.

That's the part of you that I'm reaching out to right now. In order to access that part of yourself on a regular basis, there's a ritual you must engage in that will allow you to expose and to expand that unlimited potential that you have within you to do more, to have more, and to experience more. Let me remind you of the story I told about George Bernard Shaw, who was a thought leader in his day, recognized for his accomplishments and for his brilliance. He was asked this question by a reporter. "If you had it in your power to come back and be anyone throughout history, who would you like to become?"

As you may remember, Shaw replied, "I'd like to become the man I never was." Wow. Now I want to ask you a question. I'm sure you've done things that you feel good about, things that you've accomplished that you can pat yourself on the back and say, "I've done something good." We've all done that, but let me ask you something. If you had your life to live over again, could you have done more than what you've done thus far? Absolutely, you could. If we are honest with ourselves, all of us will have to say, "Yes, and why don't we?"

Well, studies indicate that eight to nine out of ten choices that we make every day are not made by the conscious mind. They're made by the subconscious mind that is formulated between the ages of zero and six. We determine what's available to us and what's not available to us. I believe that we have to engage in a ritual, a process, on a day-to-day basis to access that subconscious mind, that part of ourselves that we have lost touch with because we live in a world where we're told more about our limitations than our potential.

The world gives us the belief systems that we have and the level of expectations that we have, and that's how we begin to operate. That's why my favorite books says, "Be ye not conformed to this world, be transformed by the renewing of your mind." We earn within $2,000 to $3,000 of what our closest friends earn. Why? Because we're affected by our relationships, by our environment. We don't even realize it. I want to talk to you about a part of you. It's that intangible part of yourself that we don't speak of.

I was reading a book called *Positivity* by Dr. Barbara L. Frederickson. In this groundbreaking work she talks about the times in our lives when we feel connected to others, we feel loved and feel playful and creative, or silly. Or when we feel blessed, and at one with our surroundings. Of this she wrote, "When your soul is stirred by the sheer beauty of existence, or when you feel energized and excited by a new idea or a hobby, positivity rains whenever positive emotions like love, joy, gratitude, serenity, interest, and inspiration touch and open your heart." She goes on to say, "Positivity opens us. The first core truth about positive emotions is that they open our hearts and our minds, making us more receptive and more creative."

I want you to engage in a process that will allow you to practice certain principles of positivity. What do I mean by this? Well, when you face a rejection, there's an emotional response to that. Every negative response that you have to a rejection or anything else in your life, you need to have at least three positive things, a positivity quotient to offset that. Yes. As you begin to look at your goals and dreams now, we're going to deal with that part of who you are behind the selling strategy, that part of yourself that exists behind your approach to your plan of action, your energy—your whole field, your whole vibration on how you show up and how people respond to you.

Now this is something very exciting. Let me share it with you. When you have this kind of mindset that I'm talking about, when you're engaging in a ritual that involves first, that you get up each day and before you do anything, you begin to monitor this program that you will have created for yourself. Start doing some things that will help to build up your spirit. Start doing and listening to things that will feed your mind, feed your faith, and allow your doubts to starve to death. Get up in the morning with a spirit of gratitude; that you're just grateful to be here.

I remember calling a friend of mine named Mrs. Williams. She is the mother of my mentor, Mike Williams. She's in her eighties. I said to her, "Mrs. Williams, how are you doing today?"

"Child, I'm doing great," she replied. "I went to the bathroom by myself and I told myself I'm grateful."

I told her, "TMI—too much information." But you want to start doing things that you're grateful for. Just waking up with no pain in your body's a good thing. Waking up in the morning, knowing it's a great day. Any day above ground is a good day. If you don't think every day is a great day, try this; it will work.

You want to laugh at yourself. You want to challenge yourself. You want to see life as an adventure. Helen Keller said, "Life is either a daring adventure or it's boring," and I'm saying to you, start a ritual. Just get in the habit of doing some things that will make you feel good every day. This is your time. This is your ritual to empower yourself. Why? Because you're going to take some hits. Things going to happen to you in life and there's a reason my favorite book says that you must pray unceasingly, because things are going to happen to you personally and professionally. They're going to blindside you. Many times you won't see them coming. One phone call can change everything. One phone call can change the chemistry in your body. One phone call can drop you to your knees. One phone call.

I'm telling you what I know: that you have to have a program for yourself. It might be writing down seven things that you're grateful for when you first wake up in the morning. I'm grateful for the ability to hear. I'm grateful for the ability to move around and not have pain in the lower part of my body. No matter what's going on with you, you want to focus on the things that you are grateful for. The ability to use your talents, abilities, and skills. The ability to have the personality and charisma, and the presence to attract customers and to close deals, and to grow your business. The ability to be a blessing to others, to help doctors to grow their practice, and to serve their patients, and to enhance their patients' health, and to save their lives.

What a powerful blessing and force you are on the planet. Just think about that, that you're a blessing. That you're a blessing to others. Have that kind of mindset and be grateful for the little things in life. It's amazing if you just start doing that. Why is it important? Because we are all affected by CNN, Constant Negative News, day in and day out. People are concerned about the seasonal flu every year, but they need to be concerned about the mind flu every day. Every day our thoughts are contaminated. Every day the words that are spoken to you affect you or infect you in a negative way. You must have a program to live your life from the inside out. Words are powerful and the words that you say to yourself are important.

When you see certain situations are so very important, these are times when people have to become very vigilant about what they're saying to themselves, about what's being said to them and said around them. These are some incredible times. We're living in a time in which we know anything is possible, yet there's still an undercurrent of fear and uncertainty, an anxiety that a great deal of people are experiencing. The suicide rate is off the charts for young people between ages 14 and 25. Right now is an incredible time, and we have to begin to monitor ourselves and speak affirmatively to ourselves.

This is the time you want to engage in *conscious languaging.* Conscious languaging first in what you say to yourself. Psychologists might call this your self-explanatory style. Let me give you a case in point, one of the mind viruses that infected me as a speaker, as a trainer, as a professional, and as a platform seller. I was doing a tour with a group of speakers. Donald

Trump was one of the presenters on this program. The program was called *Millionaires in Training*. Now, the mind virus on the tour that I was infected by and so was everybody else, is that no one wants to be the last presenter at the end of the day. Why? Because at the beginning of the day, let's say there are about 3000 people there. Usually there are about six or seven presenters each day, and we all had to close and sell a certain amount of product. Well, at the end of the day, the audience would probably fall off to be about—say if you have 3000 people, maybe at the end of the day, around five o'clock, there may be 200 to 300 people left.

The mindset was that by five o'clock most of the money had been sucked out of the room. The mindset was that when you are at the end of the day, all that's left is the crumbs from the table. All the money is gone. People were tired and worn out after hearing all these talking heads, and the money had left the room.

Now I want to talk about the gentleman who came after everybody. Believe it or not, his name is James Smith. That's his name. He wasn't bothered by that. He didn't ask to come on earlier. James Smith's mindset was, "This is the best group of people here." James Smith's mindset was, "There's more money in this 250 or 300 people than in all of the 3000 people that were in the room." James Smith's thinking was, "There's money in this room and I'm going to get that money before it leaves here." This blew my mind. I had heard about him, and I stayed to watch him on many of the trips to cities we both went to. I didn't always stay but I stayed and I watched him.

He's a curious person to me to this day. He's different. He broke all of the rules of selling and presenting and talking to the public. He would come up and say, "Some of you all need to leave here right now. You are only here to suck up and to Trump. You are not a player, you're a spectator. You need to pack up your stuff and leave right now. You could—because I don't want you running out of here screaming. Yes, that's right. I'm talking to you." Sometimes he would point out people in the audience. He'd say, "You know what, when you are talking to a group of people, you should not talk about politics. Well, I'm going to talk about politics." He'd say, "You know, you shouldn't talk about race." Then he'd say, "I'm going to talk about race."

This guy broke all the rules. He was arrogant. He was political. He was controversial, but let me share something with you. Let me tell you something. When James Smith coughed, the presenter of this seminar, the promoter, the man who put the money up, would run and get cough drops, hot tea with honey and lemon, or whatever James Smith needed. You know why? Because James Smith sold more products than all the rest of us combined.

I don't feel good saying this, but he blew me away. I was embarrassed. I was in a state of shock. I was in awe. I said to myself, *How does he do it?* I wanted to know him. I realized that as I got closer to him and we became friends, that he didn't like everybody, but I was very fortunate that he liked me. He admired me and he was open to working with me. He knew I was curious about him, and I wanted to study him because you see, I believe if anybody can do something, I can do it. He put his pants on one leg at a time just like I do, and I just couldn't handle this guy eating my lunch every day. I couldn't handle this guy selling five to ten times more than I did every day.

The other guys just chalked it up as a fluke. They thought he was lucky or that he was different. And he was different, but let me tell you something. I found out as I watched him that it wasn't all about strategy and skill. Let me tell you what it was. It was who he was behind the words. He just believed his mindset. He came in with a mindset and looked at the audience like the only reason they were spared from birth control was to buy his product; to do what he told them to do. There was arrogance in him and there was a belief and an expectation that "I'm going to suck the money out of this room. Everybody in here is going to buy from me." He would close on over 80 percent of the people in the room. They would run to the back of the room and throw him their credit cards.

I'm telling you what I saw. I sat there with my mouth wide open, eyes wide open, and I just said to myself, *Oh my God*. It was who he was behind the words. He believed. He believed that he was the best seller on the planet. He believed that the product he was offering was better than my product and Donald Trump's product, and the products of all the other presenters on the platform. He believed that he was the answer and that he had the answer to all of the problems that the people in the audience were facing. They would run and go to the credit card machines and hand over their credit cards, and call family members and friends to come by and bring their credit cards to the meetings, if they didn't have enough money on their own credit card.

His package was two to three times more expensive than the packages of the other presenters. He had a different standard. He had a different mindset and he would just say, "This is what my stuff costs," while all the rest of us used cutting or slashing prices to motivate people to go to the back of the room and capture this deal that's available today and today only. "You can't get this on our website; you've got to get it now," to create urgency. But James Smith would say, "I don't cut my prices because I know what my stuff is valued at. I know how good it is and it will work for you."

I learned something about that. I learned something about the value of believing in yourself and believing in your product, and believing in what you're doing. I learned about that combination of believing that you are the answer and that you have the answer, and about the power of expectation. Just everything about him from head to toe, the look he gave the audience, the way he moved and walked back and forth on the stage, and above all when he spoke said "I expect you to buy everything I've got back here on this table." Yes.

You see, you don't want to go in with a mindset of expecting not to get the deal or expecting to be rejected. There's no question that rejection is out there, but there's something in you, this positive emotion, this vibration. There's something in you when you are in alignment with yourself that won't allow a person to open his mouth or her mouth and say, "No, I'm not interested." There's a dimension, there's an energy field that you can create. I'm telling you what I know.

I took the time to talk with James Smith about his personal ritual. Unlike most of the presenters or the speakers who just went out and talked, he had quiet time. He took time working with himself, working with his emotions, working with his spirit, working with his energy, working with his thoughts, being in alignment, being focused, concentrated—a laser-like approach to closing the room. He had a ritual. He listened to motivational messages first thing in the morning. Things that he read empowered him; made him feel good. Same thing with the music that he played. His exercise, his meditation, his prayer, his visualization were all part of his ritual. All of these things you must do, too. See yourself going past the gatekeepers. See yourself being confident, standing in your power as you speak and through the words that you speak, there's a spirit that will touch and transform the thinking of others. There's a feeling that they will have about you that says "Yes." They will look in your eyes and say, "Yes."

The smile that you give makes them say yes. The way that you touch their hands. The way that you hold yourself in the space. They are compelled to say "yes" to you. Everything you do, when you show up, when you get out of the car in the parking lot, tells people to say yes. Things are lined up, for your crooked places are made straight, and an environment has been created that says "Yes" to you. Yes to your products. Yes to your service. Yes to your advice. Yes. Yes. Yes.

James Smith created that ritual of yes. I worked with that and I can tell you it's been very valuable for me. Living your life from the inside out rather than from the outside in. See, most people go through life as thermometers. Like thermometers they react to the temperature of life, but the James Smiths of life are thermostats. They don't react to the temperature. They don't care about what's going on in the general economy. They are only focused on their personal economy. They don't care what people say, like "Oh well, the laws have been changed, and it's been more challenging now than ever before in this industry," and focus on all the stuff that's been taken away. They focus on what's left, and how they can maximize that. They look at what's left and say, "This is enough. I can do this. I can make this work. This is all I need. If my chances are slim to none, I'll take slim."

That's a different kind of energy. This is a different kind of peace. I'm telling you that you've got that kind of power in you. You've got the right stuff. You could feel it in me right now. You can feel it now in you. Yes, yes, yes. That power. That's who you are. When you get this, you are going to have some experiences that will amaze you. Yes, you will.

Believing. Working on that belief. Reading. Developing a ritual that feeds your spirit, that feeds your energy. Being in a positive state of mind. Living your life from the inside out rather than from the outside in. It's amazing; just think about this. We're all familiar with this story of Roger Bannister, the first person to run a mile in under four minutes. No one had done it before. They once used horses to pull men trying to do it, but once Roger Bannister did it on his own, many other individuals achieved the same goal. What changed? The only thing that changed was the belief that it could be done, and the expectation that it would be done because now everyone knew it had been done.

Here's what I want you to do. Get a ritual. It could be writing, or prayer, or meditation, or listening to audio programs for 30 minutes to an hour a day while driving around in your car. Maybe before going in to present or to see a customer you sit in your car and get centered, get into your energy and your power, and talk to yourself and say, "This is it. I'm going to accomplish some incredible things today," and visually see yourself going step by step through the process. See prospects welcoming you and telling you to come in. See the gate-keepers and the staff being nice because you showed up. See them responding to this invisible force around you that they can't explain but is so inviting and irresistible that it is an atmosphere of yes.

Visualize that. Come from your heart when you speak, not from your head. They're looking at you. When you show up, they're asking three questions: Who are you? What do you have? Why should I care? You want them to be able to discover in a positive way who you are—through your smile, through the look in your eyes, with your presence. Trust me, they will say, "Yes." It will be the greatest experience they will ever have had, and that you have ever gone through. They will say, "Yes." You will be able to serve them and help them to solve problems that have been keeping them up at night. You will have insights and strategies that will help them to grow their business and better serve their customers because you showed up. They know their lives and their business will never be the same again because of your presence.

5

SAY YES TO YOURSELF

Say yes to yourself, yes to your dream, yes to the opportunities that are before you, to better serve people. I want to focus on an area that I think is very important and that is actively working to change how you see things. When you change how you see things, you change the things that you see, as the saying goes, and how you approach things that happen. Shakespeare said, "There is nothing either good or bad, but thinking makes it so."

I want you to have a mindset and the skill-set to reduce the impact of negative things that will happen to you in life. Charlotte Joko Beck said. "Life always gives us exactly the teacher we need at every moment.

This includes every mosquito, every misfortune, every red light, every traffic jam, every obnoxious supervisor or employee, every illness, every loss, every moment of joy or depression, every addiction, every piece of garbage, every breath. Life always gives us exactly the teacher we need at every moment."

I remember early in my career there was a businessman that I had a meeting with. I got access to him to sell him on using me and my services. This person made it his business, as I saw it, to break me, to humiliate me, to anger me. He wanted me to run out of his office screaming with my hands up in the air, saying "No, I can't do this." He was really working on me that day. He knew what buttons to push. He did everything but call me the N-word directly, but he used that at the meeting as well several times. I'm telling you, I learned a lot that day, and he and I, although we started out at opposite ends of the room, became very, very close friends because I held my ground, because I didn't buy into what he threw at me, because I didn't allow myself to be a thermometer. I was a thermostat. I didn't react. I responded and I'm sure you've encountered some situations like this.

Perhaps had it been another day, he wouldn't have gotten the same Les Brown. Had it been a different day, maybe I would have broken his jaw. Had it been a different day, I might have looked at him, my eyebrows raised, and said, "You're about to make me lose my mind." Had it been another day, I would have looked at him and said, "You know, you have no idea who you're fooling with. You don't know what you're about to lose." Let me tell you something. I had to pray in the moment. Do you hear me? I mean, I wanted to sprinkle myself with some oil because this guy knew he was getting to me, and I decided to stop it. I drew the line within myself. I said, "He's trying to get to me."

Here's step number one. Things are going to happen to you in life. I mean, that's just life. Viktor Frankl calls it unavoidable suffering. Things will happen to you in life in dealing with customers, and dealing with your family members and dealing with your children, and dealing with your friends. Things will happen to you in life and you must actively reduce your negative response to those things. Number one, don't feed into it. Case in point: I was standing at a counter and the person behind the counter came up. I was the first person there. A gentleman came up to my right—in a T-shirt, mind you—and the person behind the counter looked at this gentleman, who was white, and started talking to him. After he helped the white gentleman, he walked away from the counter. The white gentleman said, "Hey, this gentleman was here first." I'm standing there with a red tie, white shirt, navy blue suit, looking presidential. I had my Barack vibe going for me, all right?

The man behind the counter said, in responding to the white gentleman, and while looking at me "Oh, I didn't see him." The white gentleman and I were a foot apart, we were talking, and yet the counter man said, "I didn't see him."

I looked at the white gentleman and I said, "You see? I'm invisible. That's why he didn't see me, so please don't blame him." Then the guy behind the counter said, "Well, it's the end of the day, and I just didn't see you."

I said to him, "Okay." Now, pause right there. There was a part of me that's like, "Excuse me. At the end of the day, your racism is so blind you that you can't see me?" Let me tell you but there's a part of me that starts feeding into that and bringing all kinds of stuff. What I had to do was to stop it.

I said to myself, "Les, no. Don't go there. Don't feed into this. Back away from it." The Temptations had a song years ago, *Just My Imagination, Running Away with Me*. My imagination. If you allow your imagination to run away with you, it will. It will feed all kinds of things into itself. It will bring up a whole lot of stuff that has nothing to do with the situation. At the end of his particular day, the guy probably was just distracted and he didn't mean any harm. Here I am, I'm about to make him a member of the Ku Klux Klan, and maybe he was a member, maybe he wasn't. But at any rate, I saw myself getting angry and I had to stop myself and say, "Don't feed into this. It's not worth it."

There's something that I think is very important in the context of things that are going to happen to us. This is worth writing down. When things go wrong, don't go with them. Don't go with them. Don't lose it. You've got to hold yourself to a higher standard and not feed into it, and keep the main thing the main thing. My friend whom I met when I was there to sell him, I had to remind myself why I was there. I wasn't there to argue with him about politics. I wasn't there to argue with him about things that we disagree on philosophically. I was there to sell a service, to provide a business proposition that could enhance and bring more money to his bottom line, and allow him to serve the people that he wants to serve. I had to keep the main thing the main thing, and I had to raise the bar on myself and raise the conversation to another plane. So when things go wrong, don't go with them. Don't feed into it.

The next thing to consider is the tendency to dispute things. It's easy to get into that because negative energy and comments are far more powerful than positive ones. It's easy to get caught up in it. It's easy to be sucked into it, and so part of what you have to do is to put things in perspective. I live by this as often as I possibly can, and it takes practice and it takes discipline. I have a friend, T.D. Jakes, who said that if you've got a problem man or money can solve, you ain't got no problem. Wow. If you've got a problem that man or money can solve, you ain't got no problem. I said to him, "You know something? Thinking about that as a 15-year cancer conqueror, thinking about that and reflecting on the fact that just over a year ago I had 95 percent blockage in two of my coronary arteries and didn't know it, and that I have five stents in my heart as I talk to you now, that has a lot of power and reality for me."

Yes, it does. It's very important, and it takes practice. It takes discipline, and really I must be honest with you, despite all the practice and all the discipline, there's still some stuff that can get through to you. That can sneak up on you and you say, "Wait a minute." And that takes me to the next place. You've got to catch yourself because even with all of the practice and discipline and listening to audio programs and reading 10 or 15 pages of something positive every day, and with all the prayer and meditation, there's somebody out there that knows how to get through your armor. Trust me on this. They know how to tap your shoulder. They know how to bring it all down. They know how to make you snap.

I'm telling you, they know how to take you there and you must catch yourself. You must have the clarity of mind to catch yourself. That's why it's important

that we work on ourselves every day, that we have a ritual to insulate ourselves, to take on the whole armor of
confidence and positivity, and be able to have a spirit
of optimism and being unstoppable and relentless,
and be loving and engaging and respectful and mag-
nanimous. Understanding and knowing that it's not
personal, even though it feels personal. You are on a
mission. When you are on a mission, you must be willing to do what is required to make things happen.

You've got to say to yourself: *This can't get to me. This
is not going to stop me*. Sometimes you've got to pause
in the car, look in the mirror, and talk to yourself, and
ask yourself, "Are you going to allow this to stop you?
Get that out of your mind. Shake it off and come on.
You've got to make this happen. You've got too many
children to be stopped by this. Anger is not an option
here. Anger is the wind that blows out the lamp of the
mind. Oh no, you're hungry to get this business and
you're going to make it happen no matter how hard it
is or how hard it gets; you are going to make this sale.
Absolutely. No matter how difficult it is or how difficult
it might become, you are going to get this business."

That's the mindset you have to have. Absolute faith,
that's the kind of spirit and energy that you must show
up with, the feeling that you will not be denied. Oh no,
you are the one. You were born to do this. You've got
products that have been scientifically proven. You are

the person, you have the skills, you have the personality, you have the ability, you have the passion, you have everything it takes to build this business, to move these products, and to enhance the service they provide for their customers. You have everything you need. You're going to make this happen.

Will it be easy? Sometimes, it will. Most of the time, it won't be easy. Will you encounter resistance? Yes, you will, but an airplane can't fly without the resistance of air. You will always face challenges in life. It's called life. You have to deal with it. Most importantly, give it everything you've got. That's patience. That's understanding. That's insight. That's experience. *Give it everything you've got.* A.L Williams said, "All you can do is all you can do." All you can do is enough, but make sure you really do all you can do. Sometimes, just stepping back and being still is all you can do. Just getting quiet. Sometimes asking for help is very important. Ask for help, which most people won't do because of pride. Pride cometh before a fall because of ego. Ego means Edging God Out.

Ask for help, not because you're weak, but because you want to remain strong, because you want the business, because you've hit a wall, because you're stuck. Because you don't have the answer doesn't mean there is no answer. Einstein said, "The thinking that has brought you this far has created some problems that this thinking can't solve." Now it's about turning to the team. Turning *to* each other rather than *on* each other. Getting some other thinking involved in the process; allowing things to be seen by some fresh eyes with some new thinking can create a breakthrough for you. Ask for help, not because you're weak, but because you want to remain strong. Find out what are the best practices that are being used. How did someone else facing this same situation overcome it? Try that, and if that doesn't work, go back to the drawing board and find out what else can you do, because somebody's going to get the business, and it might as well be you.

Absolutely the business will be gotten and that business has got your name on it. That money's got your name on it. You are a professional. You have to hold yourself to a higher standard. Don't allow somebody to trivialize you and make you feel like a chump. Absolutely not. It's not that kind of party. You're going to make this happen. You are the one to get the job done. As you learn not to feed into the problem, you learn not to amplify it and allow your imagination to run away with you. You learn how to diffuse it in your own mind. You learn how to ask for help. Understand and know this as you look at yourself, look at the goals that you want to achieve and the things that you have to overcome. There's a mindset that you have to have:

I'm the one. I'm the one. I was born to do this. I can make this happen.

The final step is to say, "I can do this." That's one of the most important things. I remember when I was told I had cancer, I said to myself, "I can do this. I can beat this cancer. I'm going to do this." I visualized myself doing it. I spoke to myself as I walked and exercised every day. I said, "Every day in every way, I'm getting better and better," and you can do that as well in selling, and in any area of your business. That's what I convinced myself of when I went and watched other people standing on the platform selling and earning thousands of dollars, and I was picking up peanuts. I said to myself, "No. I can do this. I can make this happen. I can learn this. All of us are born the same way: naked and speechless. I can do this. I can learn. I can master this."

I'm still getting better. I'm still reaching and I'm still stretching. I'm still challenging myself. See, at the end of the day you never find out how much you know until you find out how little you know. I have found I'm still discovering things about myself and my abilities and talents. As you are on this journey, you will find that there's so much more in you than you even realize. There's a line in the *Lion King.* "Simba, you are more than that which you have become." I can say to you based on my own experience: you are more than that which you have become. What you earn right now is not a true reflection of you. What you have sold so far is not a true reflection of you. It's only a tip of the iceberg of what's in you. There's more in you than you're producing, than you are manifesting right now.

Part of being able to get access to that part of yourself is to not allow the negative things that you encounter in life to sap your energy and strength and lower your vibration. Part of it is watching your energy. Part of it is not feeding into the negatives, not engaging in gossip, not buying into all the things that you hear and not believing in all the roadblocks and obstacles. Part of it is having a clear mind and being laser-focused on what you want to achieve and what you want to sell, and how you're going to serve, and that you are the one and you're going to deliver. Part of it is having to hold yourself to a higher standard in the quality of the service that you provide.

A lady was asked a question at a news conference, "How is it that you are becoming a dominant force in your industry, which has been dominated by men? How is it that you are able to overcome all of the obstacles and achieve market takeaway? How is it that with limited staff and resources you've been able to get here?" She answered, "It's not our intention to please our customers or to satisfy our customers. Our intention is to amaze them with the quality of our service." Wow. Just think about that.

When I decided to become involved in selling and speaking and presenting, my goal was to achieve something unique. As Jerry Garcia of the Grateful Dead put it, "Success is not being better than everybody else. Success is doing what you do so good that nobody else can do it like that." Yes. You should be operating out of the thinking of Henry David Thoreau, who said "Do not go where the path may lead but go where there's no path and leave a trail." You want to redefine the game, take it to another level, another place. People have to stand by and be amazed and say, "How did she do that? How did she get that business? How did he do that?" Yes, yes.

It's about holding yourself to another standard and being willing to die to who you are now and give birth to who you must become. There's greatness within you and part of releasing that greatness is not allowing the negative things to sap you of your energy and your strength and your creativity, not allowing it to tarnish your mind and your heart, not allowing it to infect you. No, no, no. You have greatness within you. Yes. Yes, you do.

6

DON'T PLAY IT SAFE

What you've done is only a tip of the iceberg of what's possible for you. You have so much in you that you're not even aware of. Leap—and grow your wings on the way down.

The reason I believe that most people never discover their greatness is that most of us go through life playing it safe. Fred Smith of FedEx said, "If you are 38 and you haven't had some major failure in your life, you haven't done anything." Eight out of ten millionaires have been bankrupt. Most people never discover their greatness because they don't want to fail. They don't want to make any mistakes. They won't want to look stupid. That was me. I didn't believe in myself and

I didn't feel I was good enough because I hadn't gotten a college education, because I'd never worked for a major corporation. I'd never done those things. And so I didn't believe in myself.

If you're not willing to risk, you can't grow, and if you can't grow, you can't become your best, and if you can't become your best, you can't be happy, and if you can't be happy, then what else is there? I love what Helen Keller said. She said, "Life is short and unpredictable. Eat the dessert first."

You're going to get hurt. You're going to get hurt in life when you go after your dream. When you have a goal and a dream that you want to achieve, you have to face the fiery furnaces of this world. Things are going to happen to you. What we must do in life is look for those things that we can be thankful for. There's something special about the spirit of gratitude. Gratitude dispels negative thoughts and negative emotions. A spirit of gratitude boosts your immune system and it gives you a sense of clarity, allowing you to begin to anchor yourself on the positives of the life rather than on the negatives. When you have a spirit of gratitude, you understand and know—as Ralph Waldo Emerson said, "What lies before you and what lies behind you is of small consequence to what lies within you, and what lies within you, that nothing that you are facing is bigger than you are."

I read something that I just love. Let me share this with you. When things happen, it is very important—and I want you to write this down—make a list of the things that you are thankful for. Why? Because life is going to catch you on your blind side. When you get on an airplane they say before you take off, "Fasten your seatbelt because you're going to experience some turbulence before we reach a comfortable altitude." Am I right on that? And so it's very important to look for ways in which we can be thankful.

I like something that Mark Twain said about being thankful, about gratitude. He said "If I were asked to give what I consider the single most important useful bit of advice for all humanity, it would be this: Expect trouble as an inevitable part of your life and when it comes, hold your head up, look it squarely in the eyes and say, I will be bigger than you. You cannot defeat me."

You've got to have a spirit of—when life calls your name and taps you on the shoulder, you've got to stand up within yourself. I remember a mentally ill man who went to a place to kill kids. I can't remember, but I think they were Quakers. The oldest kid said, "Shoot me first." And after that one was killed another one stood up and said, "Shoot me." Another one said, "I'm next."

These little kids who put their lives on the line for the smaller kids, and the older kid who did survive, who didn't get shot said, "We felt if he shot us first that someone would hear the shots and come running and save the little ones." That kind of gratitude about life and that kind of courage in the little kids who made that decision, who were unflinching in that tragic situation there that they were unflinching—I said to myself if that's available to them, that kind of gratitude, that kind of love, that kind of determination, that kind of drive, that kind of courage, it's available to us in the midst of the things that happen to us.

When the time came to say goodbye to my Mama I held her hand and said, "Mama, let go baby. You've done good by us." I remember she looked off into the distance and a tear fell out of her eye and I started thinking, *"God gave me 50 good years with this woman.* Fifty years. I feel that God took me out of my biological mother's womb and placed me in the heart of my adoptive mother. I had no right to grieve; I was thankful. A poet said, "If you but knew where I stepped, you will wonder why you wept." When you look at your life, make a list of why you're here; the things that you are grateful for. When you look back on the past year, what are you grateful for? We need that spirit of gratitude in the midst of all the things that are going on now and the things that are going to happen. Because in life you either end a problem, or leave one behind, or are headed toward one. A spirit of gratitude will fortify you. A spirit of gratitude will inoculate you and empower you to handle the hits in life. Let us all say: *Be thankful.*

The other thing that is important is to be coachable. I believe the reason most people are living a life of mediocrity and not living up to their true potential is that they aren't coachable. They are not willing to listen. Someone asked Mr. Washington, "How do you explain what Les Brown has done versus all of the other students that you've had who were much smarter than Mr. Brown? He was in special education; they made the honor roll. They went off to college, he didn't go to college. He didn't have all the things going for him that they had going for them. What is it that you would attribute his success to? Was he very talented?" Mr. Washington simply said, "No." So then he was asked, "Was he an exceptional student?" Well, of course I wasn't an exceptional student. I was in special ed. "Then how do you explain what he has done?" they asked him. Mr. Washington replied, "He listened."

Do you know people who won't listen? I'll never forget a friend of mine named Lorraine Watkins. I did an intervention for her brother, who was addicted to drugs, and he asked us to leave his house. I was walking down the steps and I said, "I'm sorry, Lorraine. I wasn't able to succeed in getting your brother to commit himself to a drug program." She looked at me with tears in her eyes and she said, "No, Leslie. You did the best you could. "I've come to realize that most people won't participate in their own rescue." Well, she was right—most people won't participate in their own rescue. They'll get angry with you when you try to give them some advice. As you look at yourself and look at your goals, understand that we only have enough energy to go so far on our own. Being in a community of achievers, being around other like-minded people challenges you, and having a coach does that too.

If you can't see the picture when you're in the frame, why do you need a coach? *That's* why you need a coach. Because a coach can stretch you and push you in areas where you can never push yourself. That's why I am who I am. Mike Williams said, "Les Brown, you can be more than a disc jockey." Had he not spoken those words to me, I would never have considered becoming an intellectual resource for corporate America. That was not part of my reality, but he saw that in me. How many of you ever had somebody see something in you? As I said, you can't see the picture when you are in the frame unless you are willing to listen.

Find someone that's doing what it is you want to do on the level where you want to be. And you might have to have a variety of coaches. I've got a spiritual coach, a physical fitness coach, a mental fitness coach, and a life coach. You've got to have coaches in your life to help you get to the next level, because this is your time. That's why you're here. This is your time. Only people with a sense of mission, a sense of destiny, will get to the next level. You need to feel within yourself that *it's time for me to make my move.*

Marian Wright Edelman has said, "In life, when you don't have enough courage or insight to know that you have outgrown a situation and it's time to move on, life will move on you." And so as you look at yourself, look at your goals and dreams, focus on the creative things that you can do right now that can take your life, your idea, your dream to the next level. Creativity must be nurtured. It must be encouraged. And through the synergy of being around other like-minded people in that mastermind environment, your creativity will stimulate you, and some things will come up for you that you would not know otherwise. When we challenge ourselves—I remember during the time when I had resigned from the Ohio Legislature during my third term to go back to Miami to take care of my mother— and there I was had to start all over again. The money that I had saved disappeared; I didn't know at the time that insurance companies have a cap on how much they will pay for medical expenses. Ninety-five percent of the people who file for bankruptcy do so because of medical expenses.

When the insurance company would no longer pay, the money I had saved disappeared like it was nothing. There I was, no college education, a former state legislator, and I had to start all over again at age 42. There's a saying, "Adversity introduces a man to himself". What is your gift? What is your talent? People had been telling me for years what my gift was. And then a fateful day came. I went to a multilevel marketing organization and I encountered a person who didn't like me (and I didn't like her), but we were still in communication with each other. I said, "Listen. I want to share something with you. I want to introduce you to an opportunity." And this person said to me, "I'm not listening to you. There you go again. You've got gold in your mouth. You need to use your gift. If you use your gift, you will never need anything else in life," and she walked away.

Now, I don't know why what she said meant something to me. Maybe because all the other people at that organization liked me, but I knew she didn't. But if she didn't like me and she still saw my gift, then I had to say to myself, "Whoa. I must have a gift when somebody who doesn't like me can see something special in me."

I'm thinking, what am I going to do? I had to be creative. And so I decided to use my time by doing voluntary work in the community, working with young people in Miami. I resigned from the Ohio Legislature and went back to Miami where I was born and raised in Liberty City, and I volunteered at the New Horizons Youth Center. I came in as a volunteer youth leader. While I was in the office of the CEO, the phone rang. I could hear the person on the phone. The person said, "Listen. They're giving out contracts at Dade County Auditorium. You want to come down and submit a contract to get this money that at 12 midnight will be going back to the federal government. Before that phone conversation even ended, I had left the room and caught a bus downtown to Dade County Auditorium.

So I'm walking around listening to people give their presentations. I'm listening as people from various organizations were getting approval for the contracts they had submitted to the county commissioners. I didn't have a contract. I just gotten the information, but I was not going to say no in the situation. Someone asked Bill Gates, "Who do you fear most? Which one of your competitors do you fear most?" He said, "I don't fear any of them. I fear two people in a garage somewhere thinking of something that I haven't thought of." I realized that some of that money had my name on it and I had to think of a way to get some of it that very evening. I didn't have time to write a proposal. I wasn't known in the community, but I wasn't going to say let that stop me. You've got to be courageous.

Yes. I think courage is the most important virtue you can have. Because if you have the talent, if you have the intelligence, if you have the gift, if you have the ability, but you don't have the courage to act, nothing happens. You have to have the courage to confront your fears as I did. For 14 years I procrastinated. I get angry when I think about it; for 14 years I ruled this life out for myself because I didn't have a college education; because I told myself I wasn't good enough; because I never worked for a major corporation. I came up with all of these excuses because I was a coward. Part of having courage is the willingness to say yes to life.

I was reading something that Paul Tillich said about courage. He said this: "I understand the courage to be as the courage to say yes to life in spite of all the negative elements on human existence; in spite of man's finitude. Which means he's coming from nothing and going to nothing to die. It takes courage to see in the reality around us, and in us, something ultimately positive and meaningful and to live with it, even love it. Loving life is perhaps the highest form of the courage to be." Loving life. Saying yes to life. I've never seen a person running into a building that was burning to pull someone out and save them. I've never seen somebody throw themselves in front of a car to push somebody out of the way and save their life; never seen that kind of courage.

The kind of courage I saw is how my mother responded when she was asked, "Would you take these children and raise them?" She had a third-grade education. She had never had any children herself and she said, "Yes, I will. I will do that." Courage is when you lose everything and you don't give up. The most courageous acts are never witnessed. Courage is when you say to yourself, "I'm going to make it no matter what. No matter how bad it is or how bad it gets, I'm going to make it. I'm saying yes to my dream." Say yes.

Let's go back to the Dade County auditorium. I was thinking while I was walking back and forth. I decided not to be intimidated by the people who were coming up and making their presentations. I had to be creative. I started pacing back and forth and then I went outside to get some fresh air. There was a drugstore across the street. I heard a voice say, "Go in the drugstore." I went in the drugstore and I was walking around, saying to myself, "Why am I here?" We all have a moment in our lives when we see red light, the light changes and something says, "Wait." And then suddenly, a car comes through. And you say, "Whoa." You listened to the voice.

I'm walking up and down the aisles and a voice said, "Look to your left." There was the stationery section. I went over there and grabbed a ream of typing paper,

500 pages. Then I saw a folder. I got the paper; I got the folder. I went up to the counter paid for them. The cashier gave me my change and I said, "Do you have a rubber band?" She handed me one. And I said, "May I borrow your felt pen there?" I wrote on the manila folder, *The Les Brown Youth Enrichment Seminar.* I put it inside of the folder and I put the rubber band around it. I went in and I put my name down as one of the presenters. Then they called my name, "Les Brown, Youth Enrichment Seminar."

You want to develop your personality, a passion and your voice. I came before this group of people who were hearing the presentations and I said, "Hi. My name is Les Brown. I'm from Miami originally, and I've been listening to the programs designed for young people. I believe that as you talk about having programs to keep young people busy during the summer, your real goal is to give them the tools, methods, and techniques to make it through life. And I believe that if we can have little league football teams and baseball teams and basketball teams, then we can have little league for kids who want to become dermatologists, cardiologists, and endocrinologists, and my program is designed to do that. As you can see, this is 500 pages and it would not be cost-effective to duplicate this and give all you copies of a 500-page document.

"I will entertain any questions that you might ask," I told them. They said, "Mr. Brown, how much does your program cost?" I didn't know how to price it. The person who presented before me, gave a cost of $225,000 for their program. Now I played a card game called bid whist and players of that game say "Come high or stay home." So I told them, "$350,000."

"Mr. Brown, have you ever done this program before?" they asked me.

"No, not in terms of the kind of structure that I'm talking about. But I have lived this program, sir."

"Very good. Mr. Brown, here's what we will do. To start off with, we will give you a $100,000." We will give you a $100,000 as start-up cost." I didn't answer immediately because I didn't want to speak in unknown tongues.

I thanked them and they told me, "Go to the treasurer and get $50,000 for your staff and supplies. Go to your left, sir and get the check for $50,000 to start things up. Other people are coming up to present. We're fighting time, sir."

"Absolutely," I said. I went over there and I was watching to see if anybody followed me. They wrote me a check for $50,000. It's a true story; it's documented. When I went out to the elevator, I wouldn't get on the elevator with anybody for fear they might try to rob me.

I waited to get on the elevator by myself. When the door closed I said, "Oh my God, I can't believe it. Oh my God. This is unbelievable." I went to a payphone and called my sister. I said, "Margaret, I need you to come get me. I'm downtown at Dade County Auditorium."

"What are you doing?" she asked me.

"They gave me a check for $50,000."

"Why?" she said.

"I don't know," I replied. Oh my God. I'll tell you. I was successful. I created the program. It was my first contract and I was creative and courageous, and I made it happen.

All of us have something to give. All of us have something to share. In order to live your dream, in order to do something you've never done, you've got to become someone you've never been. There's somebody in you that you can feel; you can sense it. George Bernard Shaw talked about that person when he was asked, If he had it in his power to come back and be anyone throughout history, who would you like to be? "I'd like to become the man I never was," he said.

We can't quite put our hands on it but we feel it within ourselves, and all we need is some help. All we need is some encouragement. All we need is some inspiration. All we need is to be coached to help to bring it out. To be creative and relentless in how we use talents, abilities, and skills. Commit yourself.

When I became a motivational speaker, I caught a Greyhound bus from Miami to Dallas, Texas. At that time I didn't have any more money. The promoter said, "If you show up, Les Brown, this is the only business I know where you can earn a million dollars accidentally, if you have a passion for people and you love helping people." I get very creative and asked my friends to come by my mother's for slices of sweet potato pie that she'd make. We had dinners and I earned enough money to go to Dallas, Texas, to pay the $2,500 for the seminar.

Let me tell you, my Momma fixed me some marinated frog legs and, as God is my witness, those frog legs helped me. I was on the bus from Miami to Dallas, trading frog legs for fish sandwiches and pork chop sandwiches, for collard greens, for macaroni and cheese. It was amazing. They called me the frog man and everybody on the bus knew me. When we got to Dallas they said, "Okay, frog man. We're here." I was at the back of the bus. I got my things together, and then I said, "All right. Everybody, listen to my name. I'm Les Brown. I'm Mrs. Mamie Brown's baby boy. One day you're going to hear my name." At that point, I braced myself and I hopped out.

As I hopped into the terminal, everybody on the bus laughed so hard. The bus driver couldn't pull up, he was supposed to leave because he was running late. He said, "Wait a minute, I got to take up a love offering for this guy." He took up a love offering and they raised $650 for me on the bus, so that I would be able to fly back. Isn't that something? I believe in angels. When you show up, the universe will deliver angels to serve you. But you've got to show up. You've got to be committed to the idea that you're going to make it no matter what. There are some lines that Goethe wrote. I love this. I lived by this: "Until one is committed, there's hesitancy, the chance to draw back, always ineffectiveness. Concerning all acts of initiative and creation, there is one elemental truth, the ignorance of which kills countless ideas and splendid plans: that the moment one commits oneself, then Providence moves too. All sorts of things occur to help one that would never have otherwise occurred. A whole stream of events issues from the decision, raising in one's favor all manner of unforeseen incidents and meetings and material assistance which no man could have dreamed would come his way."

Whatever you can do or dream you can do, begin it. Boldness has genius, power and magic in it. Begin it now.

I once saw Dr. Norman Vincent Peale interviewed on the Robert Schuller show, *The Hour of Power*. I said to myself, "I must demonstrate this. I'm going to be on the

Robert Schuller program. I'm going to be interviewed by him." I've made a commitment. Write this down: *make the commitment.*

When I met someone I would say, "Hi, my name is Les Brown. I'm going to be on the Robert Schuller show." If they asked me when I would tell them I wasn't exactly sure. When they asked me if I knew Robert Schuller, I'd reply, "No, I don't. Do you know anyone who knows Robert Schuller?" When they'd say no, I'd say, "Okay, fantastic. If you meet someone who does know Robert Sculler, please get in touch with me. Here's my card."

I did this because I was committed. Then one day I was flying to Chicago from Detroit on Southwest Airlines. Only four people besides me on the plane. I'm seated next to a guy whose name turned out to be Lafayette Jones. So I told him who I was and went into my routine about being on the Robert Schuller show.

"When?" he says.

I said, "I don't know." I asked him if he knew Robert Schuller.

"No, I don't," he replied. Then he asked me, "What do you do?"

I said, "I'm a motivational speaker."

"You're kidding."

"No, not at all."

"Oh my God," he says. You're an answer to a prayer. I have an event at my company tomorrow and my speaker canceled. Can you speak?" Of course I said I could.

Then he said, "My boss gave Robert Schuller a million dollars. He can introduce you to him."

So I spoke at the event the next day. And after I spoke Lafayette Jones' boss, a man named Robert Johnson, got up and said, "Mr. Brown, I've never heard of you before but if there's anything I can do to help you out, please let me know."

I said to him, "Do you know Robert Schuller?"

"Oh, yes. Bob is a very good friend of mine."

I said, "I want to be on his program."

"I will make that happen," Mr. Johnson replied.

Two days later I got a call from Robert Schuller. He introduced himself and invited me to be on his show. I appeared four different times in all. I don't tell you that to impress you, I tell you to impress something upon you. And that something is when you make the commitment, when you're courageous and you show up for yourself, things will happen that you cannot begin to imagine. You must be relentless.

Be relentless.

Be thankful.

Be coachable.

Be creative.

Be committed.

Be positive.

Yes, we all must learn to be positive. Negative people will look at opportunities and all they can see are the obstacles. But positive people will look at obstacles and all they will see are the possibilities. That's what happens in this environment. Most people, because we live in a world where we're told more about our limitations rather than our potential, develop the mindset of, "I can't do this." I've had that mindset. But there are people that prove us wrong. We look at them and we say, "What do I have to complain about?" I know of someone who can't even wipe the sweat off her face. She has to find a way to make it happen, to cook, to prepare food, to take care of her child, to be a wife. She is a wife. She is a mother. She is an entrepreneur. She has made a commitment with her life, despite having no arms, no legs, a commitment to change the planet with what God has given her. Write this down: *I have more to share.*

We must be more positive. Now, in order to be more positive, we have to practice. It takes practice to be positive because we have a propensity to be negative. We don't have to motivate ourselves to procrastinate. Am I correct? We don't have to motivate ourselves to beat ourselves up and talk about ourselves. We do that easily. We don't have to motivate ourselves to have guilt, to be lazy and not driven and not inspired. Who wants to live an inspired life? I'm sure you all do. Someone said that many people died at age 25 but don't get buried until they are 65. Walking, breathing corpses. That when they die, we won't know they're dead because of the low impact of their lives. You won't know they're dead until the newspapers start accumulating and there's a stench coming through the walls. We won't know.

The other thing is to be patient. Be patient. Don't interpret a delay as a denial. Be patient. Things don't necessarily happen when we want them to happen. Sometimes a dream has a life of its own. Let us know when to be still.

Sometimes you need to be still. Sometimes the best thing to do is to be still. As we become still within ourselves and listen to the small voice within, we learn and train ourselves to block out the noise of the world and listen to ourselves. John Leslie said, "Most people are more focused on their distractions rather than their destiny." Have the courage to get still and to listen to *you*. Write this down: *I must listen to myself. I must trust myself. The answers are in me.*

Let me end this chapter by saying I don't know what your goals are, but I do know that you have greatness within you. Everything that I have said in this book, you already know. It's already in your heart, in your spirit. I am confirming and validating that which is already a part of you. Here's what I know. You've got dreams, you've got ideas, you've got inventions, you've got gifts that the world needs. Someone once said that life is God's gift to us and how we live our lives is our gift to God.

7

THE POWER OF EMPOWERMENT

Now I want to share some steps with you that are required for making it through tough times. I want you to write this down. The 10 steps I want you to practice. This is for your first 100 days of this year and beyond. Here's the first one. *Be thankful.* See, regardless of where your life is, my favorite book says, "In all things, give thanks." See, it's easy when things are going good for us to be focused on the negatives, but you want to be thankful even in tough times. There's something to be thankful for.

I'll never forget the first home I bought for my mother. We went into foreclosure because of me, because of my negligence, because of my not paying attention to the details. I'll never forget when we had to pack up and go back to the roach-infested home in Liberty City that I had so proudly moved her out of. I'll never forget the look in the neighbors' eyes and the shock of them saying, "Mamie, are you back? Are you all back?" I can still hear Mama saying, "Yes. Yes, we are. Leslie lost the house, but it's okay. We're back."

I felt so humiliated. I felt so defeated. I was at the back of the truck. I was crying and people were looking at me. I was thinking about the fact that I had let Mama down, and I had let myself down. Tears were coming down my face, and Mama came to the side of the truck. She said, "Boy, hold your head up."

I said, "Mama, I can't. I feel so stupid right now. We are right back where we started."

She said again, "Hold your head up." She put her hand on my chin. She said, "Hold your head up. You have nothing to be ashamed of. We still have each other."

That was Mama saying, "It's not about the house. We've got each other." Wherever we are in all things, be thankful. Something good is going to come out of it. You have to have that kind of mindset. We took the furniture into the house and the roaches were so glad to see us. "Mamie's back," they were saying. "We're going to have sweet potato pie. Mamie's back." Oh my goodness.

Hold your head up. Yes. Robert Schuller was right about experiencing tough times. Tough times never last, but tough people do. Here's another thing. Not only must we be thankful, we must be thoughtful.

The reason most people collapse during tough times is that they are making decisions out of their emotions and out of their fears. Zig Ziglar calls it false evidence appearing real. You want to think. This is the time for high-level thinking. You want to calm yourself. You want to get grounded and you want to think your way through this situation. Almost all of us have been here before. Adversity introduces you to yourself. You can come up with some solutions right now, but what happens is that most people, rather than thinking, they're being driven by their fears.

They're being driven by the thoughts that they are allowing to permeate their mind. The panicky thoughts. The thought that "This is the end." The story that "I can't make it, I can't see the light at the end of the tunnel." They become overwhelmed by that. That's why millionaires and billionaires are in the news for committing suicide. They're not thinking. They're taking a permanent solution for a temporary situation. Write this down: *I must think my way through.*

Here's another thing: *be active.* My mother used to say, "An idle mind is the devil's workshop." You want to be active. You want to be actively engaged in working on a solution and moving in the direction of where you want to go. A friend of mine named Matt Jones said "If you're going through hell, don't stop. Keep moving." If you're going through hell, don't stop. Keep moving. Don't stop and tell everybody. Eighty percent don't care, and the other twenty percent are glad it's you.

You should be too busy to worry, too active, too engaged in life to have room for worry. When you are active and moving, it eliminates depression. Even if you don't have a job, or you lost your job. Volunteer. Become engaged in life. Help someone. If you had some things going for you and they change, hey, it doesn't mean you're finished. Eight out of ten millionaires have been financially bankrupt. That just means that you're a millionaire in training. Monitor your thinking and monitor your words. Don't say, "I'm broke." Say, "I'm overcoming a cash flow problem." *Be connected.*

Yes, you want to buddy up with like-minded people that you trust who are making things happen. Remember OQP. Only quality people. Don't try to do this by yourself. Ask for help. Ask for help not because you're weak, but because you want to remain strong.

Ask for help and don't stop until you get it. That's what I had to do. I had to ask for help when I was diagnosed with prostate cancer. I had to talk to people. I had to reach out. The motivator needed some motivation. The things that I used to tell people to encourage and motivate them, now I needed that. Many people won't ask for help because of pride. Pride cometh before a fall. Because of ego—EGO, Edging God Out. Ask for help. There are people who will help you. If two or three people say, "No," just keep asking for help and don't stop until you get it, because I can tell you, based upon my own experience, that somebody somewhere will help you.

I've done some things and I know I didn't get where I am by myself. Some people helped me, including some people that I don't even know. People who prayed for me when they heard that I was in the hospital with five stents in my heart. I'm here because of God's grace and mercy. We're all here because somebody stood up for us, somebody prayed for us, somebody spoke a word and encouraged us. That's why we're here, so you want to be connected. You don't want to isolate yourself when you're going through stuff.

Here's the other thing. *Be patient*. We live in a time in which people stand before a microwave and tap their feet. People engage in business and after four or five months they say, "I haven't gotten rich yet." They spend 40 years on a job, the journey of the broke, and don't expect to get rich, then they go into business for themselves and expect to make it overnight. It's not that kind of party. You've got to be patient and consistent.

The bamboo tree. You probably know there's a tree called the bamboo tree. You plant the seed. You water it and cultivate the soil for five years. It takes five years for the bamboo tree to break through the ground. You want to give yourself a minimum of five years to make your dream come true. Now, with the bamboo tree, after five years when it breaks through the ground, it grows over 90 feet tall in six weeks. The question is, did it grow 90 feet tall in six weeks or 90 feet tall in five years? I say in five years because at any time had the cultivation and the watering process stopped, the bamboo tree would have died in the ground.

There are many people who decide they want to become an entrepreneur. They have the talent. They have the ability, but they don't have the will. They don't have the dedication. They don't have the commitment and they let their dreams die in excuses. They let their dreams die in rejections. They let their dreams die in "No." They let their dreams die in them. Maybe that's why Oliver Wendell Holmes said "Most men and women take their music to their graves every day." As you think about yourself and think about your goals and dreams, be patient.

Write this down: *be* persistent. You've got to come back again and again and again. You've got to be persistent. You're committed. Commitment is the willingness to go from failure to failure, rejection to rejection without losing your enthusiasm. You've got to keep your head up. You've got to know that building a business is a character-building experience. Never say, "I had a bad day today." Say "I had a character-building day." There's no such thing as a bad day. If you think there is, try missing one. All of those days that you have disappointments and defeats and setbacks, all of those painful days introduce you to yourself.

Next thing is: *be* positive. You see, a negative person can look at opportunities and all they will see are the obstacles. A positive person will look at obstacles and all they will see will be the opportunities. The thermometers out there, all they're seeing now are what the headlines say, what the stock market is doing, how many people are being laid off, how many companies are closing. That's all they are looking at right now. You want to be positive. You want to walk by faith and not by sight. You are more than a conqueror. You've got greatness in you.

I had to do this. When I had cancer and my PSA was going up, I was told it had gone from 125 to 230. I said, "Well, it's not over 300." Then it went to 400. I said, "Well, it's not over 500." I had to be positive. You want to find something positive in everything that happens to you because it's there. Write this down: *good things are supposed to happen to me.*

Let that be your affirmation every day. Every day. I say to myself, "Good things are supposed to happen to me." Every day. I remember one of the major accomplishments in my life. When it happened I said, "This is too good to be true. Something is bound to happen." And it did. "Thou shall decree a thing and it shall be established until you"—I called it forth. There are no overachievers in life. You want to affirm every day. Good things are supposed to happen to me. No matter how bad it is or how bad it gets, I'm going to make it.

That's your affirmation. Every day, no matter how bad it is or how bad it gets, I'm going to make it. That's what I said to myself every day when I would get up and go for a walk. I don't care what they say; that does not apply to me. No, no, no, no, no. I can overcome this. Remember what Ralph Waldo Emerson said: "What lies before us and what lies behind us is of small consequence to what lies within us." Or think about this line from Shakespeare: "The fault, dear Brutus, is not in our stars, but in ourselves, that we are underlings."

Elsie Robinson said, "Things may happen around us and things may happen to us, but the only things that really count are the things that happen in us." You've got greatness in you. Great is he that's in you than he that's in the world. What's in this world? Negative thinking. What's in this world? Toxic people, adversity.

What's in this world? It doesn't matter. What's in you? You've got greatness in you. You are greater than your circumstances. You are more than your portfolio, than your stock options, than your job. Yes.

You can make it happen. You can start all over again. Think about the value of knowing who you are. Live your truth. The fact that you have the ability to turn any so-called impossible situation around. Write this down: *be creative.*

This is a new era we are in. This is the era the late Peter Drucker called the era of the three C's: accelerated change, overwhelming complexity, and tremendous competition. Today, you've got to be creative. The days when you could work at a job for 40 hours a week for 40 years are gone. That's gone. Those days will never come back again. You have to have an exit plan.

You have the power to create. God made us, but we create our lives. I was going to a job that I hated every day. They didn't make me show up. No one held a gun to my head. I didn't like them and they didn't like me. They paid me just enough to keep me from quitting, and I worked just hard enough to keep from getting fired. I didn't have an exit plan. I was showing up angry, walking in asking what time it was. I would get a headache after 60 minutes just thinking about the job.

Do you know that on Monday mornings the heart attack rate increases by 35 percent between 6:00 a.m.

and 9:00 a.m.? Studies indicate that over 80 percent of people who have jobs go into jobs that they don't like. They don't like their job. On Mondays between 6:00 a.m. and 9:00 a.m. people die of heart attacks getting ready to go to jobs that they hate. Most of them die on the toilet. That's not the way to go.

Helen Keller said, "Life is either a daring adventure or it's boring." Those folks didn't die of a heart attack. Their hearts attacked *them* and said, "Didn't I tell you I don't want to go anymore?" Their hearts weren't in it. See, you weren't born to work for living but to live your making, and living your making will make your living. When you can make a difference and earn a living too, it doesn't get any better than that. You were born to do this. As we begin to reflect on being thankful and thoughtful and being active, being committed, being patient, being persistent, being positive, being creative, write this down also: *be concerned.*

You want to be concerned but you don't want to be consumed. Be concerned, but you want to seek out good information. If you don't get good information, get a subscription to *Success* magazine. Why? Because you want to study success. If you are going to go to a particular destination, but you've never been there before, what do you do? You get a map or you talk to someone who's been there. Why do we want to do that? Because we want to saturate our minds with information. You want to seek out information that can help you move ahead.

Stuart Johnson, the founder and CEO of Success Partners, has been doing this for years. Why? Because it made a difference in his life. He decided to become a distributor for good news, and here's the message that he brings: to be a light on the planet. All the thermometers out there, I guarantee that if you go to their house and if you ask to look at the magazines they're reading, they won't show you copies of *Success* magazine. Instead they'll show you all kinds of magazines about people who are living their dreams. You want a magazine that will teach you how to live your dream. You don't want to be an observer. This will make you a player.

Here's the next step: *be faithful*. Be faithful. It's easy to have faith if you have a secure job. You're earning the money that you want to earn. If your marriage is working out, if you have all your bills paid, if you have your health, if the children are behaving like they have good sense and judgment, then it's easy to have faith. It's easy to have faith then, but the true test of faith is when life knocks, when you have tribulations. Think it not strange that you will face the fiery furnaces of this world. Things are going to happen to you over the next year.

Why? That's just the way it is. Viktor Frankl calls it "unavoidable suffering." Charles Udall said something

I love. He said, "In life, you will always be faced with a series of God-ordained opportunities brilliantly disguised as problems and challenges." Be thankful. Whatever you're going through, it has not come to stay. It has come to pass. Be thankful. In all things, give thanks. When I lost my job in broadcasting, I had no idea that as a result of being fired I would become a community activist. That I would become a state legislator in the state of Ohio, elected to three terms, and got 14 bills passed in my first term.

I had no idea I would go on to produce five specials for PBS. I had no idea I would have a nationally syndicated talk show that was the highest rated, fastest canceled talk show in the history of television. Well, at least I had one. I had no idea I would become a motivational speaker. I had no idea I would become an author. I had no idea I would become a speech coach. I had no idea I would be speaking to people years later on a stage in Las Vegas.

Helen Keller said, "When one door closes, another door opens," but most of us spend so much time looking at and talking about the closed door, we don't see the open one. Forgetting those things that are behind us. Reaching for those things that are before us. We press toward the mark; our higher calling. How many of you feel that there's a higher calling on your life? I say to you that at this stage of my life, I know the only reason that I'm where I am is a higher calling on my life. I know that. I'm not a religious person. I think religious people are afraid of going to hell. Spiritual people have been there.

It's your time, and you have to act as if it's your time. How many of you believe it's your time? You need to know that it is your time. This is your time.

8

STRETCH YOURSELF

When you approach someone, two questions arise. Number one, is it worth it? Nietzsche said, "If you know the why for living, you can endure almost any how." Why do you do this? Why did you say yes to this? There's something in you that said, "What this opportunity provides is worth it for me to do whatever is required of me to build and to invest the time, the energy, to develop the skill-set and the mindset to begin to create a new chapter in my life."

It's not easy. Absolutely not. But when you find something that makes it worthwhile for you, that gives meaning and value to your life, the fact that it's not easy is no big deal. Here's the other question involved: can I do it? Have you heard people say, "I can't do it"? That's why it's very important that you are able, through your strategic message, to help them understand why it is worth it, the value and the impact that it's going to provide. Impact drives income.

After listening to them—and you have to be a good listener so that you can talk to them from a place in which they understand and can hear you—after listening to them you can, through your strategic storytelling method, talk to them from a place in which they can hear and understand you. You give them a larger vision of themselves that goes beyond their mental conditioning and their circumstances. A recent study indicates that 9 out of 10 of our choices are made by our unconscious mind. We're probably all familiar with the story involving the great anthropologist Margaret Mead, when she visited a restaurant in Europe.

A waiter approached the table and he told her that there were several Americans in the restaurant. She said, "Tell me after you serve them dessert. I can tell you exactly how many are here."

The waiter replied, "You couldn't possibly do that."

She said to him, "Just let me know."

After he had served dessert, he came over and said, "Okay, I've done it."

She got up and walked around. She observed the people eating their dessert. She said, "You have 65

Americans here." He checked the roster. He said, "How did you know that?" She said, "Because in Europe, when you eat a slice of pie, you eat it from the crust toward the tip. In America, when we eat a slice of pie, we eat it from the tip toward the crust."

Do you eat a slice of pie from the tip toward the crust? What else have you picked up? That's why an MIT study showed that we earn between $2,000 to $3,000 of what our closest friends earn. We are born into stories. There are things you've learned in life that can help people to get a larger vision of themselves beyond their mental conditioning and their circumstances.

Here's another thing. Are you coping or actively developing tools and techniques that change your life and your business? One of the things, as we begin to look at people, is that most people are volunteer victims. They complain about their situation, and I did that for years. I was going to a job that I didn't like. Nobody made me go there. But I had an excuse. "I've got to buy groceries," I said. "I've got a mortgage. I've got a car payment. I have a wife. I have children." I was using all of those as excuses for doing something I didn't want to do.

I was a volunteer victim because at any point in time, I could have made a decision that I wanted to do something else. There's a quote I love. "Wherever you find yourself at some point in time, you made an appointment to be there." I had to own that when I read it; that grabbed me. Another thing that's important: it requires ability. You can be motivated. You can have a positive attitude. But if you don't take the time to develop the ability, it doesn't matter about your mindset. It doesn't matter how motivated you are.

Think about the law of attraction. If you're not willing to work to develop that ability, all you will attract will be hard times and wishful thinking. It takes ability in order to get to where you want to go. Demand more from yourself than what you have achieved so far. *Stretch yourself.*

You have to consciously stretch yourself. It's easy to settle in. You've got to demand more of yourself each day. What am I going to do? A lady said something to me that really grabbed me. She was reflecting on the election of Barack Obama, and she said, "You know what? When I look at what he did against such incredible odds, I looked at myself. I've got to get a bigger dream. I've got to do it better and I've got to do something different."

Let me share something with you. That's where I am right now. I've got bigger dreams now. I'm still here. I still got blood flowing through my veins. There are some children whose lives I'm going to touch. I'm going to reduce the recidivism rate among people who are incarcerated. There are people that I need to talk to, to say to them, "You are more powerful than cancer." There are people that I need to talk to and say, "You can live your dream. You've got the power to do more than you can ever begin to imagine. You are not your circumstances."

I can talk to them about this because I've been there. I know what it is to settle. I know what it is to give up. I know and I can free some people up. I can say, "It's not over until you win." I can talk to people about that from a place of knowing because I've been there, done that, and bought the T-shirt. That's what people want right now. People made a choice between hope and fear. They are looking for hope. When there's hope in the future, that gives you power in the present.

Here's another thing. Discover your power of voice. You've got to learn how to tell your stories strategically to make an impact. Create a unique experience for your customers. You can't treat people like a transaction; you must listen to them. People, as they say, don't care how much you know until they know how much you care. How much you care. You've got to listen to them. Ask them questions, get to know them. What drives them? What motivates them? What keeps them up at night? You need to know these things.

You know what drives me? My children, my grandchildren. You know what drives me? I want to make a difference. My mother fascinates me. She adopted us when she was 38. I remember in her declining days as I sat by her bedside and watched her I wondered what caused her to say, "I'm going to adopt seven children." She only had a third grade education. She was a domestic worker. When I had the talk show a reporter asked her, "Why did you adopt those children?" She said, "I wanted to share my life with someone. I want to touch somebody." She never had her children herself.

When I was looking at her and thinking about how hard she worked, that's my why. What's yours? How many of you have someone in your life you'd like to do something special for? I want you to think about that person because that's what drove me. That really is what I talk about and like to find out. Create stories that people can identify with. The only way you can do that is to become a story listener; then you can speak to people where they are. Don't allow what you want to say get in the way of what they need to hear. Create a one-on-one experience. Be there. Be present.

Most people don't listen today. Once when I was in church, as I was walking past some people they said, "How are you doing?" "I'm dying," I replied. They said, "Praise the Lord. Good. Praise the Lord. Praise the Lord." So I said, "Hello? Hello? I said I'm dying." They didn't even hear me. They didn't even hear what I said. Just went on automatic. Just be present with people and show interest in them. People are looking for relationships. Look them in the eye and speak to them.

I was giving a lecture at the University of Michigan a while back. A lady wrote a letter to the president of the university, talking about a parking lot attendant she had encountered. When she came into the parking lot and was paying to park, he asked her how she was doing. She said she was coming there to have chemotherapy, and he said to her, "You're going to do just fine. Things are going to be all right for you." He didn't just take her money and say, "Go ahead." He said, "Things are going to work out for you." And when she came back and told him that she'd lost all of her hair, he said to her, "Girl, you're the only one who could carry this off. You are beautiful."

He made her feel special. In her letter she was expressing her gratitude to the parking lot attendant. None of the healthcare professionals that attended to her needs recognized her. I was in the emergency room just the other day. I called my cardiologist, told him that I was experiencing pain in my chest. He said, "For how long?"

"For the last four hours," I told him.

He said, "Les," what part of your chest hurts?"

"The left side," I told him.

Then he said to me, "Go to the emergency room as soon as possible. Where are you? Who's with you?"

"My son," I told him. Then I said, "John Leslie, tell your friend to drive me to the emergency room."

After I got there they had to give me an electrocardiogram and they took me out into the hall on a gurney. I'm out in the hall and over 50 people passed me, and you would have thought I was Casper, the Friendly Ghost. You remember the movie *Sixth Sense*, where people were invisible? I was looking at people to make eye contact. Only three people, three volunteers paid attention to me. One of them said, "Sir, would you like to have a pillow for your head?" I said I sure would, and thanked him. Out of more than 50 people, only three people looked at me and said hello or made eye contact.

Write this down: *people want to be accepted*. They want to be respected and they want to be connected. My mother said, "It's the little things in life that count." When you have meetings, just look people in the eye and smile at them and make them feel accepted, "We're glad you're here." Create that kind of welcoming experience and be respectful; listen to them. "What do you do?" How long have you been doing it? Wow, that sounds exciting." Show interest in them. Hold a conversation with them rather than just trying to sell them something.

"Let me tell you how you can get rich." No, no, no, no, no. Talk to them and let them develop a relationship with you through the conversation, through this experience that you're able to create. Then they can feel connected, a part of something big. Do you feel connected, a part of something that's bigger than you?

When you forget about you, when you're doing what you love, the money will follow. That's if you answer the call on your life. My daughter Ona used to say, "Answer the call and don't use caller ID." I knew about the call on my life for years, and I didn't answer because I didn't believe in myself. I didn't answer because I didn't think I was good enough. I didn't answer because I didn't think it was worth it or that I could do it. What is it that people experience? The answer is *passion*.

The people who are going to succeed today, the people who are going to achieve at a higher level and grow their business, the people who are going to drive the recovery and begin to reverse things almost over-night for the planet, are people that have a passion. It's the difference between being in business and business being in you. If you have passion, when you speak, people will hear their hopes and their dreams in your voice. When you speak you will impact their minds, but you will also connect with their hearts. When you speak, you will change the way they think. You'll change the way they feel, and you will change the way they behave. If you don't change the way people think, feel, and behave, then all you've done amounts to cheap entertainment. That's why it's important that we learn how to strategically tell stories, to change the way people think. That's important.

When you speak from a place of passion and optimism, when you discover your power voice, you live your life from the inside out. When you discover your power voice, you discover the power that you have within you; you realize that you're more than your job. You realize that circumstances don't determine what happens to you. You realize that you are in charge, that you come from a place different from where people are talking about the problems. You are talking about the possibilities. You see things that others can't see. When you are speaking with your power voice, you come from a place of optimism. You judge not according to appearances, but begin to see things at a higher level, from a different view. You have a larger vision of yourself. You realize that anything is possible.

I guarantee you that years from now historians will look back on this time as a time of greatness. This time will give birth to more ideas, to more inventions, to more businesses, to more entrepreneurs, to more billionaires and millionaires than the planet has ever before seen. This time will show an explosion of greatness on the planet. Trust me on this. It's not going to take two or three years. It's not. No, no. One of you could change the planet. One person.

Ralph Nader said, "Cars are not safe." He took on the automobile industry, a multi-billion dollar industry. One person said, "Seat belts should be in every car." They told him, "You can't take on the automobile industry." But today you can't buy a car anywhere on the planet without a seatbelt, am I correct? One man. One messenger. Write this down: *work*.

Not only must you have passion and optimism, but you've got to be willing to work. Work, work, work. The willingness to do whatever is required. Be open to the possibilities or reinvent yourself. Einstein said, "The thinking that has brought you this far has created some problems this thinking can't solve." You look at your goals and your dreams, and then you've got to begin. You've got to be willing to die to who you've been to give birth to who you will become. You've got to reinvent yourself.

Work. Willingness to do whatever is required. Being open to the possibilities. Reinventing yourself. Showing up at conventions. Coming to meetings. Being involved. Being engaged. Communicating with, associating with, and building an organization with kindred spirits. Now here's the next thing. As we begin to look at our goals, and this is important, write this down: *energy*.

When you are aligned with your purpose, you are not working for a living, but living your purpose. Living your purpose will make your living. There's a certain energy that you bring. Now, you don't want to convince anybody to do this. Why? Because a person convinced against their will is of the same opinion still. You want positive energy in your organization, not toxic energy. There are people that are not good for you and not good for your business. There are people that, if you never saw them again, it would be too soon.

It doesn't matter if they have the personality. It doesn't matter if they have the talent. It doesn't matter about their connections. If they don't see the vision, if they don't bring the energy that you need, and that includes energy for cooperation, an energy of "we can make this happen," leave them alone. An energy of working as a team. An energy of "we are holding to the vision." If they don't bring that energy, leave them alone.

Just find someone else. There's someone waiting for you right now that you can grow with, that you can expand with. You want to be very careful of the energy around you. There's a new term in psychiatry called relational illness. There are some people that aren't good for you. "Well, can I change them, Les?" No. It's a full-time job changing yourself. There are some people that are so negative, they can walk into a dark room and begin to develop. I love that. Write this down: *relationships*.

People are looking for relationships. People will do more for a relationship than they will ever do for money. How many of you have had that experience? Relationships are crucial today, even or maybe especially in this high technology age, the age of e-mail, Twitter, and all that stuff out there. I'm not technologically adept at all. My kids sold my two 8-tracks on eBay, against my will and without telling me. Good working 8-tracks, too. That tells you I need some help. I like to hear a voice. Don't e-mail me. I want to hear you speak.

It's commonly believed that opportunity knocks on every door. I'm here to tell you that it does not. Opportunity stands by silently, waiting for us to recognize it. You want to begin to be on the lookout, have your antennas up, looking to create opportunities. George Bernard Shaw said, "The people that make it in this life, they look around for the circumstances that they want, and if they can't find them, they create them." You want to drive a recovery. You want to create a rebound. You want to help people begin to see their opportunity in you when you speak, just being in your presence. They need to know that you have something special and that you can help them begin to realize that they have something special. That they have greatness in them.

There's a difference between coming into a room and entering the room. When you come in, because of who you are, what you represent, and the work that you've been doing on yourself, people must know something great is about to happen, just because you showed up. Yes, indeed. Write this down: *ideas*.

What are the things you can do right now? Challenge yourself. Think. Robert Schuller was right: there's never a shortage of money or opportunity, just a shortage of ideas. Albert Schweitzer was asked a question, "What's wrong with mankind?" He said, "Mankind simply doesn't think. People don't want to think." There are some ideas that are lying dormant in your mind right now that the world needs. You've got greatness in you, and to prove it, you were chosen one out of 400 million sperm.

There's something in you. There's something that you have. There's something about you. There's something you showed up with, a dream, an idea, an invention, a capacity for leadership, a voice that the world needs. We need all that right now. There's a calling, a higher calling on your life. That's why you have not settled for a job. That's why you've decided, "I know I can do better than this." That's why you have not surrendered to your circumstances. That's why you're not sitting around looking at the news, biting your nails, and worrying. You are actively engaged and making things happen in your life.

People that you come in contact with experience you as you speak. They're experiencing your energy.

As you speak and connect with their minds and their hearts, they have an experience that changes that negative conversation and story they believe about themselves. You change how they feel about themselves, and their life and their dreams. You empower them to the point where they say, "My life is worth it. I deserve better than this. I can do this. I know I've never done it before, but I can do this. I know I tried in the past and failed, it didn't work out, but I can do this." You create that kind of experience for them.

My mother is what drives me. This woman who scrubbed floors and cleaned toilets. Who cooked for the families she worked for, and we ate the food left over from what she had cooked. This woman who cleaned house and made beds and looked after children. I feel like Abraham Lincoln, who said, "All that I am and all that I ever hope to be, I owe to my mother." I feel like something I once wrote, "God took me out of my biological mother's womb and placed me in the heart of my adopted mother."

What is your why? Is it worth it? I can tell you, all the effort, all the defeats, all the rejections, all the people that said no to me, all the people that laughed at me—I can tell you it was worth it. I remember when I was driving around a very affluent area of Miami, and I said, "Mama, look at that house over there," because even after we lost the first home that I'd purchased for her, I never gave up on my dream. I had a vision and I would drive through the wealthy neighborhoods every day because I knew I was going to come back. Write this down: *I have comeback power.*

I had a setback. Willie Jolley, who's a great author and speaker, said, "A setback is a setup for comeback." You have comeback power. I didn't stay home feeling sorry for myself. I didn't stay home feeling depressed. I didn't spend time telling people about the home I bought for my mother and then lost, about the guy who didn't do a title search. I didn't do a title search and it turned out there was a lien against the property, and the seller didn't tell me and so I got ripped off. I didn't spend time talking about what happened. I was actively working to get the money to buy her another home. I would drive through the affluent areas and look at these big, beautiful houses. I took my mother along, and she just said, "Whoa." I said, "Look at that one over there." And she said, "If I lived in something like that, I'd feel like Mrs. Rockefeller." So I said, "Thank you, mama."

I got out of the car and I took a picture of the house. I put it on my refrigerator. I put it on my mirror. I looked at it every day. I wrote down, Matthew 7:7, *Ask and it shall be given. Seek and you shall find. Knock and it shall be open. For everyone who asketh shall receive. He that seeketh shall find. Knock and it shall be open.* Do that. Write that down on a three-by-five card, and put your goal on the other side. Every day I looked at the picture, reinforcing it in my mind. I gave thanks that I had it. Finally, after working relentlessly, putting all my time and energy into the effort, I was able to buy the house. And then I got mama in the car, and we drove past it again.

I said, "Mama, look at that house over there again. I know the people there. Let me take you in to meet them." Many of you may have heard me tell this story before.

She said, "Okay, Leslie," and I drove up onto the driveway. Mama was 75 at that time. I went around the car and opened the door to help her out. As we were walking toward the house, she said, "Leslie? Boy, you sure you know these people?" I said, "Yes, Mama, I do." We got to the door, and I couldn't hold back any longer. I took out the key. I put it in the lock, and I said, "Turn the key, Mrs. Rockefeller. This is your home."

She said, "Leslie, what are you talking about, boy?" I said, "Mama, look," and I turned the key. I pushed the door open and said, "I bought this for you, baby." She looked at me and she stuck her head in the door and said, "Anybody home?" I said, "No, Mama. It's your home now. It's fully furnished." She said, "You know, I thought you were up to something when you took me to the furniture store and asked me what I would like." I just said, "Yes, ma'am."

As she was walking around, I stood there watching her and all I could think about was when she used to take us downtown when we were kids. Wesley would be on the right and I would be on the left, and mama walked real fast with her shoulders back. We would try to keep up with her. That was all I could think as she was walking around and looking at the house, and she said, "Thank you, Jesus. Who would have thought that something like this would happen to me? Leslie, you didn't have to do this." I said, "I know, Mama, but I wanted to."

Who'd have thought that a little sugar candy boy would win the Golden Gavel award? I produced eight specials for PBS. I once went into a meeting and the guy speaking was boring, so boring that the room was as quiet as a graveyard between funerals. He said, "I know I'm boring. I know I don't have energy. I know I don't have passion, but the reason I'm standing up here and you are seated out there, is that I represent the thoughts you have rejected for yourself."

Whoa. "I represent the thoughts you have rejected for yourself." Your top achievers, the top performers, the people that are building the business, that are taking it to the next level, the people that are making an impact on the planet, the people that are helping people achieve a vision of themselves beyond their job, see themselves as entrepreneurs. The people that can make things happen are the people who have told themselves, "I can do this." They represent the thoughts that we have rejected for ourselves.

Don't judge yourself based upon what you have done up to this point. Don't underestimate who you are. Do you know who's looking back at you when you look in the mirror? You were chosen to do great stuff. That's why you are here.

I want you to invest in yourself but I also want to tell you why I do what I do. I was born to motivate people. I was born to speak. I'm cancer-free, I'm debt-free, and I'm drama-free because of God's grace and mercy. I want to leave this with you. A friend of mine had an angioplasty, and one stent put in, and he died within 24 hours. I have five, but I'm still here. It's because my work is not through yet.

My work is not through. I believe there are people that I'm supposed to speak to, that I'm supposed to connect with. I want to leave this with you, something that I'm known for. My mother used to love to have me say this. I dedicate this to you, and to your dream. In this hour, we need you. In this hour, we need your voice. You have something special. You have greatness within you. My mother used to say, "Leslie, say that thing for me, boy, that makes me feel better." I dedicate this to you and to your dream, but I say simply this.

If you want a thing bad enough, then go out and fight for it, work day and night for it; give up your time, your peace, and your sleep for it. If all that you dream and scheme is about it, and life seems useless and worthless without it, and if you'd gladly sweat for it and fret for it, and plan for it and lose all your terror of the opposition for it, and if you simply go after that thing that you want with all of your capacity, strength and sagacity, faith, hope, and confidence and stern pertinacity, then you will get it. If neither cold, poverty, famine, nor gout, sickness or pain of body and brain can keep you away from the thing that you want; if dogged and grim you beseech and beset it, with the help of God you will get it. God bless you.

9

HAVE A VISION

I want you to write down the letter V. It stands for *vision*. I want you to have a vision of yourself beyond your circumstances. Where do you see yourself going? Don't restrict yourself; be unlimited. Here's what we know. We're living in a time in which we know anything is possible. Anything. Don't rule anything out for you. Because you can't see it doesn't mean you can't do it. We must call forth those things that be not as though they were.

The people that you talk to: you are giving them an opportunity to create a new life for themselves. As you speak to people you are speaking to the invisible. You are calling for something that they can't see right now, physically. We have been conditioned in a belief that if I can see it, I believe it. No. If you believe it, you can see it. You've got to hold this vision of yourself beyond your circumstances and make it a *big* vision. I've found that most people fail in life not because they aim too high and miss. No. Most people fail in life because they're just like I was for so many years. Aim too low and hit, that's what I did. I was hitting those low targets. Here's something else. Write down the letter E. E stands for *empower*.

Empower yourself. You've got to take the time every day to program your mind. There's a reason my favorite book says, "Be now conformed to this world. Be transformed by the renewing of your mind." There's a reason for that. Why? Zig Ziglar, the number one motivational speaker on the planet, said "People say motivation doesn't last. There's no reason to listen to motivational messages. There's no reason to go to seminars and workshops because they don't last." Zig then went on to say, wisely, "Neither does brushing your teeth last. Neither does bathing last but you do it every day. If you don't, they'll stop inviting you to parties."

You have to literally program your mind. One of the transforming moments of my life was going with my mother when she went to work. Mama worked on Miami Beach and we ate the food left over from the families that she cooked for. These were very kind and generous people. They said, "Mamie, whatever food is left over after we eat, you pack it up and take it home to those children that you have adopted." As you know, I was born in the poor section of Miami called Liberty City, on the floor of an abandoned building. Liberty City is often in the news for negative reasons. We wore the hand-me-down clothes of the children that mama took care of, and if the clothes were too small, mama would let them out. If they were too large, she'd take them in. My mother could bake, too. My mother could bake a sweet potato pie so good; you couldn't even eat it with your shoes on, 'cause your toes would wiggle too much.

When I was going to work with mama I used to say, "Mama, when I become a man, I'm going to buy you a big beautiful home just like this. My mother didn't know where those thoughts came from. "Leslie, you don't have to do that," she'd say. "I know, Mama, but I want to," I'd tell her.

One person we worked for was a Mr. Zadorsky. I had to attend to his needs. People thought he was very rude and belligerent when he spoke to me. "Leslie," he would say, "Come in here, young man. Look at this bookcase. You know I don't like dust. Dust it off. I want my shoes shiny. Do you understand?" Look at this ash tray," and so on.

"Yes, sir. I do apologize. I will take care of it, sir." That's how I'd respond to his criticism.

I loved Mr. Zadorsky. Yes, he was arrogant. Yes, he yelled at me. But he was justified because I didn't clean his room as well as I could have. I did this deliberately. I wanted to be in the room with him because every morning when he rose and went into his office, he would listen to Dr. Norman Vincent Peale. "You can't allow your negative thoughts to hold you back. You must control your thoughts or thoughts will control you." Every morning he listened to Earl Nightingale, who said "We become what we think about. All of us are self-made but only the successful will admit it." Mr. Zadorsky was programming his mind. That was his hour of empowerment, every day. This man was a multimillionaire.

I remember Mr. Zadorsky saying to his son David, "Do you want to be successful like me?" Yes, the son replied. "It takes three things," Mr. Zadorsky told the boy. "Rule number one, watch wealthy people and do what they do. Rule number two, watch poor people and don't do what they do. And rule number three, go back to number one." All of the homes that my mother worked in as a domestic worker, dusting and cleaning and caring for the children, while I was raking the yards, they all had libraries and they had personal empowerment books and recordings that they listened to everyday. Faith comes by what? Hearing and hearing and hearing.

We live in a world where we're told more about our limitations than our potential. How many of you have been told you couldn't do something? MIT did a study that indicated that if I say to you, "You can't do that," then someone else has to come along and say, "You can do it," to neutralize what I said. That's why every day we must have the discipline to focus ourselves and listen to motivational messages, in order to program ourselves for success. Now write down the letter M. M stands for *make something happen*.

You must have a vision of yourself in the future, where you're going, and take the time to empower yourself by programming your mind, because you don't get in life what you want, you get in life what you are. The next thing is that you've got to make something happen. The reason that most people are running around being fearful right now is that they're spending too much time focused on the negative, focused on things that will take their power away. I had something happen to me that no one would ever want to happen. Three words that were said to me years ago that no one ever wants to hear: "You have cancer." Three words. Cancer, the most feared word in many different languages. No one ever wants to hear those words.

I can tell you from personal experience how powerful those words are. When I was told those words, I became active trying to find people who had had those words spoken to them but were still living. What did they do? Because I knew that if they could do it, then it was possible that I could do it. Does that make sense? Yes.

I became active in seeking out solutions rather than being consumed by the problem that I was faced with. In my research I found that more people die from a doctor's prognosis than from the disease itself. That's why you have to have a vision of yourself. I had a vision of myself being cancer-free. Today I'm cancer-free, debt-free, and drama-free.

To God be the glory. And so you have to have a vision of yourself and where you're going. Never say "I'm broke." Say "I'm overcoming a casual problem. Don't say "I was fired." No, you were released so you can do what you were supposed to do. I had to make something happen. I became engaged in doing the things that would allow me to strengthen my immune system. I had to fight this fight at the cellular level. I had to change my thinking. I had to become involved in prayer, in meditation and in the visualization process. I listened to motivational messages on a regular basis so that I could strengthen myself and fight the cancer from the inside-out rather than accepting this stuff from the outside-in. Does that make sense? Yes.

The other thing is, as you begin to look at your goals and dreams, not only must you have a vision and hold that vision because you can have a lot of things happen to you, but that vision becomes your reason for being. I say in one of my motivational series, "If life knocks you down, try and land on your back because if you can look up, you can get up." Your reasons, your vision will help you get back up again. Every day you must empower yourself, taking the time to listen to motivational messages that can change your thinking. Because at the end of the day, you don't get in life what you want, you get in life what you are. Your state of mind is so important. Most people are fearful right now because they don't take the time to work on their mind.

Write this down: *monitor your mind and your mouth.* Monitor what comes into your mind every day, because it will affect you. When someone says something negative to you, such as "You are terminally ill," the capacity of your immune system to protect you drops by 40 percent. Death and life is in the tongue. Watch what you allow to come in your mind. When people tell you that you can't make your business grow, you just back away. Don't argue with them. Say, "Excuse me, I can't grow from that." Then walk away. Avoid negative people and negative conversations. It's very important that you do this. You want to be busy doing things, making things happen.

Somebody once said there are three kinds of people. Those who watch things happen, those who make things happen, and those who don't know what happened. The majority of people are looking at CNN. They're looking at NBC and ABC; they're looking at television. They're reading the newspaper to find out what's happening. You don't want to do that. You don't want to act like them. Why? Because most people live their lives on the outside; they are thermometers. They're reacting to the news. Three things you can do: you can react, you can respond, or you can initiate. You want to initiate. You want to have a vision of where you're going. You want to work on yourself, you want to make something happen, you want to master your communications skills so you can tell a story to distract, dispute, and inspire.

Remember the story I told about Mr. Washington? I'll never forget that day. I was in his class waiting for another student when Mr. Washington told me to solve a problem on the chalkboard. I told him I couldn't because I wasn't one of his students. He said, "Young man, go to the board and work the problem out anyhow." I said I couldn't and the other students started laughing and calling me DT, the dumb twin. And I said to Mr. Washington, "Yes sir, that's me."

Well, he came out from behind his desk and looked me straight in the eye. "Don't you ever say that again," he told me. "Someone's opinion of you does not have to become your reality." That was a huge turning point in my life.

Distract, dispute, and inspire. When I would come home after getting into a fight, Mama would say, "What happened, Leslie?" I'd tell her, "They called me DT." Gently she would admonish me, "Leslie, sticks and stones can break your bones, but words can never hurt you." But words do hurt. They hurt and they can hurt deeply. Am I correct?

Mr. Washington was a communicator. He was a speech and drama teacher. He delivered a strategic message when he said, "Young man, someone's opinion of you does not have to become your reality." That distracted me from what I believed about myself, that I was the dumb twin. That strategically caused me to begin to overcome the possibility blindness—that because I wasn't as smart as Wesley, didn't get the grades that Wesley and Margaret Anne did, didn't mean that I was a bad person or a dumb person. I was inspired to start a new chapter in my life. That's what people are looking for from you. To distract them from the story that, "I can't do this. I have never done this before." They can't see themselves beyond a job that's the journey of the broke.

And here's the other thing. Write down the letter A. It stands for *alliances with positive people*. The reason that most people are not achieving their goals is because they have alliances with people who have dreams that are very small, or no dreams at all. Dr. Dennis Kimbro said, "If you are the smartest one in your group, you need to get a new group." You want to develop alliances with people that you can learn from. People that can help you grow. People that are top performers in your area. You want to look at them and find out what do they do to be so successful.

I wanted to be around Dr. Norman Vincent Peale. I wanted to be around Tony Robbins and Zig Ziglar. I listened. I studied everything Earl Nightingale has said, and Jim Rohn and Mark Victor Hansen and Jack Canfield. I've been students of all of them. I've been studying them for years. I've read a lot. I've read thousands of books. I read two or three books a week. Why? Because I have this vision of where I'm going. Now write this down. Tonight, take the time to write down a clear description of the kind of person that you must become in order to produce that vision that you have of yourself. People always ask what a new president's first 100 days will be like. Here's my question to you, what will your first 100 days be like? What's your plan of action for your life?

I saw this movie *About Schmidt* with Jack Nicholson. It grabbed me; I saw it four times, but the fourth time I heard something at the end of the movie that I had missed. I don't know how I missed it, but I got it the fourth time. Jack Nicholson's character was writing to a little boy in Africa named Ndugu who he had sponsored, and he expressed his frustrations and disappointment with his life and the fact that his marriage didn't work out, and that he didn't have the career success that he desired. There he was communicating with this little boy who probably didn't understand what he was talking about.

So he says to Ndugu, "Ndugu, when you die and everyone you know dies, unless you have done something significant with your life, it will be as if you were never born." Think about that. When you die and everyone you know dies, unless you have done something significant with your life, it will be as if you were never born.

My daughter Ona, who is a motivational speaker, called me the other day from Atlanta. She was in traffic and she said, "Dad, how are you doing?"

"Fine," I said. What are you doing?"

"Well . . . oh, wait a minute." A police officer had apparently driven on a motorcycle into the middle of traffic to stop the traffic. She said, "Oh, a funeral procession is about to come." How many of you ever had that experience?

We were chatting and then she suddenly said, "Oh, whoa. Ooh, dad."

"Baby, what happened?" I asked her. Was there an accident?"

"No," she said. "A funeral procession just came by and there are only three cars behind the hearse. Whoa, "I want more people to show up when I die. I want to make an impact with my life. I want the undertaker to cry when I go."

You see, there are some people who because they didn't have a vision beyond their circumstances, because they didn't take the time to work on their mind, because they were not able to communicate their story, and didn't have alliances with positive people who could motivate them, encourage them—they didn't make an impact with their lives. That's why it's very important that you have alliances with positive people who have drive and passion; that have a purpose in life. You don't want to be a person who when they die the only way we know that they're gone is because they didn't answer the phone over a period of days, or the newspapers gathered at their door, or a stench came through the walls and the neighbors complained to the police department. That the impact of their lives was so insignificant, so miniscule.

When as I was at Cedars-Sinai Medical Center, just reflecting on my life and saying to myself, "What are you going to do now, Les?" I got a wake-up call. A friend of mine, Mel McDougall, left a message on my phone,

"Les, live each day as if it were your last because one day it will be." See, nobody's figured out how to get out of here alive. Had I died of a heart attack, I would've been the most surprised person in the room. I said, "Oh, my God." We should all remember: no regrets.

Cornell University did a study with people in their eighties. They asked them, "When you look back over your life, what do you see and what comes up for you?" Over 80 percent of them said they had regrets and more regrets; there were things that they wanted to do that they hadn't done. Things that they attempted to do but failed because they weren't committed. They tried and stopped, or they encountered a few disappointments, a few failures and they quit. Let me say to you, stand up for your dream. The majority of people, the thermometers out there, if you tell them they can't do something, they stop. They become disempowered, disoriented, and they give up on themselves, on their dreams, and they adopt a defeated mindset, "I can't do it." Write this down: *stay the course*.

I'm saying continue to say yes to your dreams, yes to that new life, yes to this opportunity, yes to the future. And if you do, you can feel special about the fact that you made a decision on your own behalf. A great person said, "I choose not to be a common man. It's my right to be uncommon if I can. I seek opportunity, not security. I do not wish to be a kept citizen, humbled by having the state look after me. I want to take the calculated risk to dream and to build, to fail and to succeed. I refuse to live from hand to mouth. I prefer the challenges of life to a guaranteed existence, the thrill of fulfillment to the still calm of utopia. I would never cower before the master, nor bend to any friend. It's my heritage to stand erect, proud, and unafraid to face the world boldly and say, 'This I have done.'"

Be uncommon. Be different. You're a thermostat. You are not a thermometer.

10

THE POWER OF FAITH

Have absolute faith and if you don't believe in yourself, believe in somebody else's belief in you. Sometimes you have to borrow somebody else's faith until your faith kicks in. On that fateful day when Mr. Washington looked at me, he looked at me with the eyes of Goethe, who said, "Look at a man the way that he is, he only becomes worse; but look at him as if he were what he could be, then he becomes what he should be." And when I heard Mr. Washington's words I thought *Oh God, I hope he is right*. You must have absolute faith. Don't worry about what you don't have. As George Washington Carver said, "Do what you can where you are with what you have and never be satisfied." I remember when I was competing for a $300,000 contract at Procter & Gamble. I was sitting across from two individuals who were there competing for the same contract, and they didn't know I was there for that reason. They were talking among themselves and they pulled out a sheet of the presenters and then they saw my name. One of them said, "This guy, he has no credentials. Between the two of us we have a PhD and an MBA from Harvard. We're going to take him out."

Sometimes life can frighten you. Sometimes life will intimidate you. Write this down: *sometimes you've got to talk to yourself.* I got up and I went into the bathroom to talk to myself. Sometimes that will be the only intelligent conversation you can have. Sometimes you've got to build yourself up. I went to the bathroom and started talking to myself while walking back and forth. I looked at myself in the mirror and said, "Les Brown, what do you care about all of their PhDs and MBAs. You are Mamie Brown's boy. You've got seven children that you've got to feed and a mama to take care of. You're like Leon Spinks. You've got no driver's license, no tickets. You have nothing to lose."

I walked into that room and I looked at the man who was supposed to award the contract, and my concentration as I looked in his eyes was, "The only reason that you were spared from birth control was to give me this contract." I got the contract and I hired them as my assistants. I'm telling you that based upon my own experience, you have greatness within you. We are designed for greatness but we are not pre-destined for greatness. That's a choice. Choose ye this day, whom ye shall serve. I hope you have some ambitious goals. My first major goal was to buy my mother a home. That was important to me. I felt like Abraham Lincoln who said, "All that I am and all that I ever hoped to be, I owe to my mother." That gave a focus for my life. Have an ambitious goal, a goal that will challenge you. T.L. Osborn said, "Unless you attempt to do something beyond that which you've already mastered, you will never grow." You want to put yourself on the path of growth, of seeking out new horizons, of testing yourself, of finding out what you are made of.

Most people go through life working at jobs where they get paid just enough to keep them from quitting and they work just hard enough to keep from getting fired. You've got to have some ambitious goals. Scrip-ture says, "Hearing my father glorify that ye bear much fruit." It could have just said, "Ye bear fruit," but it says "much fruit." What you've got to do is look at your life. You want to take life on. You want to challenge your-self. You want to go beyond your comfort zone. Why? Because that's the only way that you're going to dis-cover your specialness. You've got to be willing to give up who you are for what you can become. You've got to be willing to work on yourself.

Here are some ways in which you can do that. One is you must have ambitious goals that you think about, that you focus on, that you're reaching for. You want to read something positive every day; at least 10 to 15 pages of something positive every day, and also listen to something inspiring every day. Why? So that you are not being conformed to this world, but are being transformed by the renewal of your mind every week. Renewal or renewing, that's the key word. Every day, you want to renew your thoughts. Why is that important? It's been said that all of us are six inches from success. That's the distance from one ear to the other.

You've got to develop your mind, folks. When you have these goals that you're working on, you're focusing your energy. You begin to improve your attitude about yourself. Is that important? Most certainly. Someone did a study of some top achievers around the world, some 3,000 of them, to find out what was the common denominator that enabled them to reach their goals. They discovered that 85 percent of them reached their goals because of their attitude, 15 percent because of their aptitude. I spoke at Harvard not long ago. I have no college training. I know two people who graduated summa cum laude from Harvard, but I sign their paychecks.

Attitude. Don't be intimidated by what other people have. Just come with what you have. Do the best that you can with what you've got; that's what's important. What is it that you want to stand for? What is it you want your life to represent? As you look at the goals that you want to achieve, here's a crucial question. You've got to ask yourself, "What kind of person must I become in order to do that?" Why is that an important question? Because—and this is worth writing down—you don't get in life what you want, you get in life what you are. What kind of person must you become? Assess yourself. What are your strengths? What are your weaknesses? How is that you've been flaking out on yourself? What are your shortcomings? What is it that you know you've got change about you as you look at where you want to go?

Write this down. *Make discipline a major force in your life.* Honor your word to yourself that you'd be further along in life. Somebody once said, "Where you find yourself at some point in time, you made an appointment to be there." Now, whatever this goal is that you want to achieve, make your move *before* you're ready.

I'll do it when things get better. I'll do it when I can spell able. I'll do it when the children grow up. I'll do it when I get my divorce. I'll do it when I get some more money. Make your move before you're ready. Why? He said, "Prove me now herewith and I'll pour you all the blessing you have not room enough to receive." Prove me. We are more than a conqueror. The only way you can be a conqueror is you have to go through something. Most people are always getting ready, and they continue to procrastinate. "I'm not good enough." I said. "I don't have a college degree. I never worked for a major corporation. I don't have the contacts. I don't have the money. I've never done it before." For 14 years I did that. Don't try and figure out how you're going to do it. How you're going to do it is none of your business.

Let's go back to the book of life. It says, "Lean not on thy own understanding. In all ways acknowledge him and he shall direct thy path." I'm telling you based on my own experience. I'm telling you what I know, not what somebody told me. I'm telling you what I know: When you take that leap, the net will appear.

Leap and the net will appear. Somebody once said, "Just hit the sidewalk, man." No, no. When you get out there you want to follow your heart and not your head. I was trying to figure it out and I wasted a lot of emotional energy trying to figure this thing out. Let me tell you something, there is no logical, practical explanation for what I do; me being a person who was born in Liberty City on the floor of an abandoned building. If my birth parents came in now, I would not know them. Being labeled educable mentally retarded, failing again in the eighth grade, having no college whatsoever, never worked for a major corporation, yet I earn more in one hour than 90 percent of the American public earns working for a whole year. There is no logical, practical explanation for it, other than God.

That's what *call* means. You must have the faith to call forth those things that be not as though they were. Most of us go through life holding back on ourselves. I'm telling you what I know. I remember a point in my life when I said, "Lord, there's got to be more." I was working at a job where I was miserable. I'll never forget I came home one day, at that time I was married, and I said, "That guy I work for is stupid." My former wife said, "If he's so stupid why does he sign your paycheck?" You see why I divorced her?

I couldn't sleep that day. Winston Churchill said, "The truth is incontrovertible. Malice may attack it, ignorance may deride it, but at the end, there it is." Thomas Carlisle said, "Truth crushed to earth shall rise again." The book of lives says "You shall know the truth and the truth shall set you free." I said, "She made a very good point," and I made a decision. Make a decision about your life. A man was passing by a house one day. People on the porch were talking and as he passed by, there's a dog on the porch moaning and groaning, and the man was curious about this. He came back and asked the folks on the porch, "Why is this dog moaning and groaning?" One of people said, "He's lying on a nail."

The man was surprised. "He's lying on a nail? Why don't he just get up?" Man on the porch said, "It's not hurting bad enough for him to get up." How many of us know people who do nothing but moan and groan about their relationships? Or moan and groan about their job?

A friend of mine called me. She was crying, and she said, "They laid me off." I said, "Why are you crying? Didn't you tell me you hated that job? They didn't lay you off, they released you so you can find your own good."

Helen Keller said that when one door closes, another door opens, but we spent so much time looking at, crying, and complaining about the closed door, we don't see the open door. Charles Udall said, "In life you will always be faced with a series of God-ordained opportunities, brilliantly disguised as problems and challenges."

Now here's something else that you have to do. Three last points. First, whatever goal you have, go all out. Give it everything you have. A man by the name of Art Williams wrote a book called *All You Can Do is All You Can Do, and All You Can Do is Enough*. But make sure you do all you can do. Give it everything you have. Pull out all stops. Hold yourself to high standards. I like a quote I saw the other day that said, "Do not go where the path may lead, but go where there's no path and leave a trail." Make failure your friend. Don't worry about making mistakes; you're going to make them. Don't worry about getting hurt, because you're going to get hurt. Why? Because life is painful. Viktor Frankl calls it "unavoidable pain," because in life you are either in a problem, or just left one, or you are headed toward one.

Life is painful. I used to have a talk show. It was the highest-rated, fastest canceled talk show in the history of television. I was embarrassed. I was hurt. I was humiliated when they had my show taken off the air because I refused to do shows about fathers who sleep with their 14-year-old daughters and things like that. I refused to do that filth and garbage. So they said, "You're out of here."

When I'm walking down the street people will say to me, "Hey, didn't you used to have a talk show? They took you off the air, didn't they?" When I say that's right, then they ask, "Why did they fire you?"

I always reply, "Why don't you call them and ask them?" Somebody else will say, "Hey, didn't you used to be Les Brown?" I tell them, "I'm still Les Brown."

I was humiliated. I was hurt. I was angry. I was disappointed. But I didn't die. Nietzsche said, "What does not kill me makes me stronger." My son, John Leslie, when he was nine years old I bought him a game called a Connect Four. I taught him how to play and I then I beat him 15 straight games. At the end of the 15th game, you're not going to talk a lot of trash. Instead, I stood up and yawned and said, "John Leslie, I'm tired of beating you. Dad is ready to go to sleep now." John Leslie jumped up and said, "Oh, no dad. You can't stop now."

"Why not?" I asked him.

"Because it's not over until I win."

So he and I just kept on playing. I said to John Leslie, "Let me tell you something now. I'm not going to give you any breaks, young man. Long as you sit here, I'm going to wear you out."

"Dad, just keep on playing," he replied.

I said, "Look, I'm not just number one in Detroit, I'm number one in Connect Four all over the state of Michigan. Do you understand that?" He tells me to stop signifying and just play. I beat him five more times. At that point I told him, "John Leslie, I just got a telegram from the president. I'm number one in Connect Four all over the United States."

He said, "Dad, just play."

I beat him eight games and then I said, "John Leslie, they know my name on Jupiter and Mars. The master of Connect Four." He tells me to just play. I beat him 10 straight games, but in the 11th game John Leslie won. He stood up and yawned and said, "Okay, dad. I'm ready to go to sleep now." What if all of us had that unstoppable spirit in pursuit of our goal? You're going to face rejections again and again and again. You're going to get involved in office politics. People are going to judge you because of your personality. Folks are going to work against you. Doors will be closed in your face. You're going to face rejection constantly. Maybe creditors will be breathing down your neck. Your house in foreclosure. Car's been repossessed. People that you were counting on to help you saying you can't do it. There are times when you will doubt yourself and just when you're about to give up, deep down inside, you'll hear this small, still voice that says, "It's not over until I win." It's not over.

I'm not through yet. I'm still breathing. It's not over. No. No, no, no. You see, most people don't reach their goals; most people are wimps. It takes everything in you to go from here to up there. You're going to go through some turbulence. What's the first thing they tell you when you get on an airplane? Before they take off, what do they tell you? Fasten your seat belts. Fasten your mental and emotional and spiritual seat belts because you're going to experience some turbulence before you reach a comfortable altitude. It's okay. It's not over until you win. One last point: whatever goal that you have, you've got to be hungry.

Mr. Washington said to me, "Mr. Brown, what do you want to do with your life?"

I told him, "Mr. Washington, I'd like to buy my mother a home, sir."

"How do you plan to do that, Mr. Brown?"

"Well sir, I'd like to be disc jockey."

To this he said something I'll never forget. He said, "You start practicing and training yourself every day. I want you to visualize yourself being a disc jockey. I want you to claim it. Speak the word. "Thou shalt decree a thing and it shall be established unto you." I want you to put together jingles and radio commercials in radio format."

I said, "Wait a minute, hold it, Mr. Washington. I want to be a disc jockey. I don't have a show yet. Why should I do these things?"

He quoted Whitney Young: "It's better to be prepared for an opportunity and not have one, than have an opportunity and not be prepared." He said, "You've got to be hungry, young man."

"What do you mean by that, sir?" I asked him.

He replied, "The people that are hungry are willing to do the things today others won't do in order to have the things tomorrow that others won't have. Are you hungry to get that house for your mother?"

"Yes, sir, Mr. Washington. I promised her, sir. I promised mama. When people were telling her to take us back to the welfare department before she adopted us, I promised her that when I became a man I'd take care of her. That when I graduated, I would set her down. She would not have to be washing somebody else's dishes anymore. She wouldn't have to clean anybody's house. She'd only cook for us, sir. My Momma would only fix sweet potato pie for us."

I started practicing and drilling myself every day and finally I went to see him. He said, "Are you ready, young man?"

"Yes, sir," I told Mr. Washington.

"You got to be hungry, young man," he said to me. "Don't you know that being a disc jockey is a glamorous job? There are many people who have more credentials and experience than you have who would love to be behind a microphone and have thousands of people listening to them. But if you're hungry, the odds don't matter. The dream is big enough. You don't care nothing about the odds."

"Yes, sir," I said. And he sent me on my way.

I went to apply for a job at radio station WMBN. Milton Butterball Smith was the man I talked to. "Hello, Mr. Butterball," I said. "My name is Les Brown, sir. I'd like to be a disc jockey."

"Young man, do you have any college education, or any background in broadcasting or journalism?"

"No, sir. I don't, sir. But I'm good, sir, if you just give me an opportunity to audition for you. I'll never be able to get any experience if I'm not given a shot, sir."

He said, "I'm sorry but we don't have any job for you." I went back and I told Mr. Washington. He said to me, "Don't take it personally. Most people are so negative they have to say no seven times before they say yes." He said, "Go back again." So I did.

So I showed up at Butterball Smith's office again. "Hello, Mr. Butterball. How are you, sir? My name is Les Brown. I'd like to be a disc jockey."

"Weren't you here yesterday?"

"Yes, sir."

"Didn't I tell you no yesterday?"

"Yes, sir, but I didn't know whether or not somebody was laid off or somebody got fired since yesterday, sir."

"Nobody was laid off or got fired. Now, get on out of here."

I came back again the next day and said the same things I'd said before. "I know what your name is" he says. Weren't you here the last two days?"

"Yes, sir."

"Didn't I tell you no the last two days?"

"Yes, sir. But I didn't know whether or not somebody got sick or somebody died, sir."

"No one got sick or died. No one was laid off or fired. Now, don't you come back here again."

I came back the next day like I was applying for the first time, talking loud and looking happy. "Hello, Mr. Butterball. How are you?"

He looked at me with rage in his eyes. But he said, "Go get me some coffee." And so I did. My mama said sometimes you have to stoop before you can conquer. I became the errand boy for the disc jockeys; their little flunky. I would go get their lunch and their dinner, and I'd come in the control room and not leave until they stopped asking me to. I'd watch them moving their hands on the control board and memorized their movements. Pretty soon they trusted me to pick up entertainers that came into town. Entertainers like Diana Ross and the Supremes, The Four Tops, The Temptations. I'd drive them all over Miami Beach in the disc jockey's big long Cadillac. I didn't have any driver's license but I was driving like I had some.

Then one day I was at the radio station and a jock by the name of Rockin' Roger was drinking while he was on the air. He was slurring his words and it was obvious he couldn't complete his show. And there I was looking at him through the control room window—young, ready, and hungry. I was saying to myself, "Drink Rock, drink." I would've gone on in and given him some more if he'd asked me to. Pretty soon the phone rang. I answered it and it was the general manager. He said, "Young man, this is Mr. Klein."

"I know, I said."

"Rock can't finish his program. "Will you call one of the other DJs in?" So I said sure. I hung the phone up and said to myself, "He must be thinking I'm crazy." I called my mama and my girlfriend, Cassandra, and said, "You all come out on the front porch and turn up the radio. I'm about to go on the air."

I waited for about 20 minutes and then I called Mr. Klein back. I said, "Mr. Klein, I can't find nobody."

"Young man, do you know how to work the controls?" he asked.

"Yes, sir."

"Then go and segue the records and don't say nothing, right?" I couldn't wait to get old Rock out of the way. I got behind that turntable. I said, "Look out, this is me, LBPPP. Les Brown, your platter-playing popper. There were none before me and there will be none after me, therefore that makes me the one and only. Young and single and love to mingle, certified, bona fide and doubly qualified to bring you satisfaction and a whole lot of action. Look out, baby. I'm your love man." I was hungry. I was very hungry. You've got to be hungry.

For those of you who want to live life to the fullest, I say you've got to be hungry. You got to be willing to do the things that the others won't do in order to have the things tomorrow that others won't have. You've got to be willing to work on yourself. I say to you that whatever you've done up to this point is just the tip of the iceberg. I say to you that you are designed with greatness but not predestined for it. It's your choice if you want to have more life. No matter what you've done, I want you to know that you can do infinitely more. If anybody had told me, based on my life, that I'd be doing this, I probably wouldn't have believed them. If my birth parents showed up now, I would not know them. I was born in an abandoned building on a hot linoleum floor. I have no college training. If anybody told me I would be doing this—well, it's quite a story, isn't it?

Does it happen overnight? No. Is it easy? No. Easy is not an option. It just isn't. It's hard. But let me tell you, it's worth it. It's worth it. Your life is worth it.

Dr. Martin Luther King, Sr. put one of his sons under the best tutelage, under the best ministers and best mentors. He sent him to Morehouse College where Dr. Benjamin Mays, a great motivator, was the president. But Dr. Mays sent the young man to his mentor, Dr. Howard Thurman, a great man, a great mystic, a great philosopher, a great mind. Dr. Thurman wrote *Disciplines of the Spirit*, *The Centering Moment*, and *The Sound of the Genuine*.

In one of those books he wrote, "The ideal situation for a man or woman who dies is to have family members around them and praying with them as they cross over." He went on to say, "But imagine if you will, being on your death bed and standing around your bed the ghost of the dreams, the ideas, the talents, the abilities given to you by life and that you, for whatever reason, didn't use them, didn't pursue those dreams. And there those dreams, those talents, those abilities, those gifts, those visions are standing around your bed looking at you with large angry eyes saying, "We came to you. Only you could have given us life and now we must die with you forever." The question becomes, if you die today, what dreams, what gifts, what abilities, what talents, what skills will die with you?

Myles Munroe, a great minister from the Bahamas, said "The wealthiest place on the planet is not in the Middle East where they have oil underground. It's not in South Africa where they have diamond mines. The wealthiest place on the planet is in a cemetery, because there you'll find books that were never written; speeches that were never given; workshops that were never conducted; business ideas that were never acted on; songs that were never sung; instruments that were never played." You survived one out of 400 million sperm, you were born to win.

I leave this with you whatever your goals may be. My mother used to love to hear me say this. She passed years ago from breast cancer. She loved this. I want you to know that you have greatness within you. If you want a thing bad enough then go out and fight for it; work day and night for it; give up your time, your peace, and your sleep for it. You will gladly sweat for it and fret for it and plan for it, and lose all your terror of the opposition to it. And if you simply go after that thing that you want with all of your capacity, strength, and sagacity, faith, hope and confidence, and stern pertinacity, with the help of God you'll get it. If cold, poverty, sickness or pain of body and brain can't keep you away from the thing that you want, if dogged and grim you besiege and beset it, with the help of God, you'll get it.